THE BOOK OF

REGIONAL AMERICAN COOKING

HEARTLAND

T H E   B O O K   O F

REGIONAL AMERICAN COOKING
HEARTLAND

BEATRICE OJAKANGAS

Photographed by
GLENN CORMIER

HPBooks
a division of
PRICE STERN SLOAN
Los Angeles

ANOTHER BEST-SELLING VOLUME FROM HPBooks

HPBooks
a division of Price Stern Sloan, Inc.
11150 Olympic Boulevard
Los Angeles, California 90064
© 1993 Price Stern Sloan, Inc.

By arrangement with Salamander Books Ltd.

10 9 8 7 6 5 4 3 2 1

Photography by Glenn Cormier
Food Stylist: David Pogul
Assistant Food Stylist: Alba Cera

Library of Congress Cataloging-in-Publication Data

Ojakangas, Beatrice A.
    The book of regional American cooking. Heartland / Beatrice
Ojakangas ; photographed by Glenn Cormier.
        p.   cm.
    Includes index.
    ISBN 1-55788-073-5 : $11.95
    1. Cookery, American—Midwestern style. I. Title.
TX715.2.M53043 1993
        641.5977—dc20   93-2088
                                                                                      CIP
Printed in Hong Kong

NOTICE: The information in this book is true and complete to the best of our knowledge. All recommendations are made without any guarantees on the part of the author or Price Stern Sloan. The author and publisher disclaim all liability in connection with the use of this information.

Special thanks for props to: Penny Lakes, Bo Danica, La Jolla; Anne Hakes, Williams-Sonoma, San Diego; Susan Bass, Old Town Pottery, San Diego; and Gayle Kellner, Bazaar del Mundo, San Diego.

CONTENTS

A M E R I C A N

INTRODUCTION

The cuisine of the Heartland, or the Midwest, is all that is basic. It is like the "sensible shoes" of one's wardrobe. The Midwest has often been described as the breadbasket of the United States. Here is where fields of grain ripple in the summer sunlight, where vegetables of all varieties are grown both in family gardens and commercial truck farms, where cattle graze on the prairies and turkey and chicken farms produce great quantities of poultry for the market. In Western and Southern Minnesota and Iowa, hogs are raised in immaculate barns ending up in lean, tender pork cuts on the market. In the Red River Valley of Minnesota, potato farmers carefully guide their crops into top grade produce. And, in the north, where once iron mining was the most important industry, inactive open pit mines have been turned into huge fish tanks filled with pure, sparkling water to produce salmon, trout and other fish for the market.

Midwestern cooks have always been talented in producing jams, jellies, syrups and other preserves from the bounty of the fruits and berries in their region. Small producers of these delicious preserves sell their wares in specialty gift shops in the area. Visitors can buy thimbleberry jam, ground cherry preserves and wild grape and apple wines. Wisconsin has become well-known for its cheese production, breweries and sausages; Michigan for its cherries; Iowa for its corn; and Northern Minnesota for wild rice. When visiting any of these areas, one is always tempted to step into the local shops and sample the wares.

The Midwest itself extends from Lakes Superior and Michigan, across Minnesota, south to the prairie and plains states of Iowa, Ohio, Kansas, Nebraska, Missouri, Illinois and Indiana. Early pioneers migrated from New England in the 1700s, followed in the 1800s by ethnic settlers. Germans, Swedes, Danes and Norwegians settled in the rich lands of the Mississippi valley. A little later, after the rolling farmlands had been homesteaded, Finns, the Cornish, Slavs, Czechs, Polish and other Eastern Europeans settled the wooded, hilly, sometimes rocky areas of Northern Minnesota, Wisconsin and Michigan.

While Southern and Southwestern American foods are easily defined, Midwestern foods are not. Each ethnic group that settled in the Midwest brought with them its ethnic traditions and melded together favorite foods so often that more than one ethnic group may claim the same recipe. This is not surprising because in the world of cuisine there are many basics that closely resemble one another. Stews, soups, pies, meat dishes, dumplings, breads, pastries and desserts are basic Midwestern favorites. Their preparation, apart from ingredient variation, is similar. Transplanted into the bounty of the rich farmlands and waters of the Midwest, the original recipe, be it a rye bread from Scandinavia or Germany, or a fish stew from Southern France, is interpreted through the use of local ingredients.

Perhaps the best known contributions from Native Americans to Midwestern cuisine are corn and wild rice. Corn is not only a major crop in Iowa but essential to American agriculture.

Ingredients

FRUITS & BERRIES

Apples
Apples are grown throughout the Midwest in dozens of different varieties. Apple festivals are common throughout the Midwest in late September and October, when apples are ripe.

Wild & Domesticated Berries
Blueberries, raspberries, strawberries, elderberries, chokecherries, blackberries, gooseberries, currants and in certain areas whortleberries, high bush cranberries, ground cherries and thimbleberries are gathered from the wild as well as grown in backyard berry patches. Midwestern cooks use these berries in pies, jams, jellies, fruit syrups and sauces.

Wild & Domesticated Fruits
Apples of many varieties, tart and sweet cherries, cranberries and plums. Dried cherries are produced in Michigan and are used in baked goods as well as sauces and desserts.

Dried Cherries
Dried Pitted Sweet Bing Cherries are a delicious new cherry product which has been used in baked goods as well as sauces and desserts.

Dried Cranberries
Often called "craisins," they are available throughout the year, usually in the produce department of supermarkets. Craisins can be substituted for raisins in baked goods.

FISH

Bass
A general term for a game fish belonging to the freshwater sunfish family, characterized by its spiny fins.

Catfish
Catfish is fished in the Mississippi River and its tributaries. The fish, from its natural habitat, may have a "muddy" flavor because it is a bottom-feeding fish. Catfish are also grown on farms. Farm-raised catfish have a delicate, clear flavor. They are available in most fish markets both fresh and in frozen packages and range in size from six to eight ounces to about one pound.

Coho Salmon
A variety of high-fat freshwater salmon caught in Lake Superior and Lake Michigan. The fish can grow up to 50 pounds, but the most usual size is less than five pounds. It has a firm texture and pink to red-orange flesh. This salmon is being farmed in Northern Minnesota in freshwater tanks that were formerly open pit mines.

Herring
Freshwater herring of two varieties are fished from Lakes Superior and Michigan. Cisco herring is the fattier variety; Bluefin herring is leaner. Both are used for pickling, however, many prefer to pickle the Ciscos. Both varieties are excellent when smoked. The fish range from eight to twelve inches in length and usually weigh eight to twelve ounces.

Lake Superior Trout
A freshwater fish sometimes called "salmon trout" which, like Coho Salmon, is found in the Great Lakes but now is being farmed. Flavor is like that of salmon, size range of the fish is similar to salmon.

Lutefish or Lutfisk
A fish popular among the Scandinavian population, traditionally eaten during the Christmas season. Lutefish, or Lutfisk, is cod which has been treated with lye, dried and reconstituted in fresh water before preparation. It has a distinctive flavor, texture and aroma.

Tilapia or Perch
A freshwater fish, a game fish; it is now being raised on fish farms and may be labeled "Tilapia" or "Perch." It is available fresh or frozen in fish markets or in the fish and seafood section of supermarkets. The fillets are approximately six inches long.

Walleye
A variety of perch called "pike-perch." A freshwater fish that is probably the most popular of game fish. It is usually broiled or sautéed.

Whitefish
A member of the salmon family, this high-fat, freshwater fish is found in lakes and streams throughout the Midwest. The whole fish usually weighs from two to six pounds and is sold whole, filleted or smoked. The fresh fish can be poached, baked, broiled or grilled.

MEAT & POULTRY

Beef
Beef production has always been an important industry in the Midwest. (The National Livestock and Meat Board, representing both beef and veal, is situated in Chicago, Illinois.)

Lamb
Produced in Iowa and Wisconsin.

Pork
Pork production is a major meat industry in the Midwest. Pork produced in Minnesota and Iowa is lean and free of trichinae. Pork is packaged in more boneless small cuts than ever before, which makes the cooking of pork more convenient than ever. (The National Pork Council is situated in Des Moines, Iowa.)

Veal
Veal is produced in the Midwest, and because of its high protein and low fat content is coming into greater popularity today.

Venison
Venison cannot be purchased in meat markets as it is strictly a game meat, except for imported farm-raised venison. Deer hunting season is in the autumn.

Turkey & Chicken
Turkey and chicken producers in the Midwest market turkey in small-serving cuts. Boneless chicken and turkey breasts, turkey tenderloins, sliced turkey breast, ground turkey, turkey and chicken wings, legs and thighs are convenient for single meal and small-family use. A variety of turkey hams, smoked and roasted boneless turkey breast put turkey into the luncheon meat category.

GRAINS

Corn
A gift of the Native Americans, this versatile plant is the foundation of many popular foods. Cornfields are abundant in Southern Minnesota, Iowa, Illinois and Indiana.

Cornmeal
Used to make cornbread and corn muffins as well as batters for many fried foods.

Popcorn
A popular Midwestern snack that is grown in Iowa, Southern Minnesota, Illinois and Indiana.

Wheat
Both Spring and Winter Wheat are major products of the Midwest.

Wild Rice
Wild rice is a seed-bearing grass historically harvested by Native Americans. Through the process of selection, wild rice production has been developed so that cultivated rice in man-made paddies will produce rice that matures all at one time. Native Americans still harvest "lake rice," which requires several rounds of gathering wild rice from marshes, since in nature it does not all ripen at the same time. Wild rice goes through an extensive processing procedure to result in the grain that can be cooked.

CHEESE

Wisconsin is one of the major cheese producing states and duplicates cheese varieties from all over the world. Dairy farms are found throughout the Midwest.

Colby
A cheese named after the town of Colby, Wisconsin, where it was first made. It is a mild, whole-milk Cheddar-type cheese with a soft, open texture. Most often it is used for eating out of hand, with crackers or with sandwiches.

Maytag Blue
A type of blue cheese produced in Iowa.

SEEDS & NUTS

Sunflower Kernels
Sunflowers are grown throughout the Midwest. The kernels of their seeds are packed with flavor as well as protein.

Hazelnuts or Filberts
Also known as filberts, hazelnuts are one of the most popular varieties of nuts in the Midwest.

Other nuts grown and sold in the Midwest are black walnuts, hickory nuts and hickans.

Bell Pepper Antipasto

1/4 cup extra-virgin olive oil
2 garlic cloves, minced
2 cups white onion, diced
1 each large green, red and yellow bell peppers, diced
1/2 cup chopped celery
2 large tomatoes, diced
1/2 cup green olives, chopped
1/2 cup ripe olives, chopped
2 tablespoons capers, rinsed and drained
2 tablespoons red-wine vinegar
1/8 teaspoon each salt and black pepper
French bread, thinly sliced and toasted

Heat oil in a large skillet over low heat. Add garlic and onions; cook 10 minutes. Add bell peppers and celery; cook 5 minutes.

Add tomatoes with juice, olives, capers, vinegar, salt and black pepper; simmer 15 minutes. Remove from heat. Cool to room temperature. Serve in a small bowl or mound on toasted slices of French bread.

Makes about 6 servings.

COUNTRY CHEESE TARTS

Press-in Pastry:
1-1/2 cups all-purpose flour
1/4 teaspoon salt
1/2 cup corn oil
1/4 cup iced water

Cheese Filling:
1 tablespoon butter
1/2 cup sliced green onions, including tops
2 eggs, slightly beaten
1 cup (4 oz.) Cheddar cheese, shredded
1/2 cup half and half

Preheat oven to 400F (205C). Prepare pastry: Combine flour and salt in a medium-size bowl. Whisk oil and water together in a small bowl; stir into the flour mixture. Press 1-inch balls of dough into each of 30 miniature muffin cups to cover bottom and sides evenly. Bake 12 minutes or until edges are lightly browned.

Prepare filling: Melt butter in a small skillet. Add the onions and cook 5 minutes over medium heat or until onions are softened. Mix onions with the eggs, cheese and half and half in a medium-size bowl.

Spoon mixture into baked tart shells. Bake 20 minutes or until filling is set.

Makes 30 tarts.

COUNTRY PÂTÉ

8 pitted prunes
1/2 cup dry sherry, warmed
1 pound lean bacon
1 large onion, quartered
1 garlic clove, minced
1/3 cup vermouth
1/4 cup fresh parsley, minced
1/2 teaspoon each dried leaf sage, thyme,
    savory, oregano, salt, nutmeg and pepper
2-1/2 pounds ground pork and beef (total)
1 (8-oz.) pkg. garlic/herb cream cheese

Add prunes to sherry and let stand 30 minutes. Line a 9" × 5" loaf pan with half the bacon. Preheat oven to 375F (190C). Process remaining bacon, the onion and garlic in a food processor until smooth. Add vermouth, herbs, spices and sherry from the prunes; process until blended. Combine bacon mixture with the meat in a bowl and blend well. Pat half the mixture into bacon-lined pan.

Place a row of prunes down the center; top with remaining meat mixture. Fold the overhanging bacon over the meat. Cover tightly with foil. Place into a larger pan; add enough boiling water to come halfway up loaf pan. Bake 1 hour 45 minutes. Drain pâté and cool. Place a weight on top of the meat; refrigerate up to 2 days. Whip cheese in a small bowl until fluffy. Remove bacon from pâté. Frost with cheese.

Plum Chutney: Combine 1 (8-oz.) can plum preserves, 1/4 cup each chopped almonds and dried currants, 2 tablespoons red-wine vinegar and 1/2 teaspoon curry powder in a small bowl.

Makes 8 to 10 servings.

PIROSHKI

4 ounces bacon, chopped
8 ounces lean ground beef
1 medium-size onion, finely chopped
8 ounces mushrooms, chopped
1 tablespoon tomato paste
1 teaspoon dried leaf thyme
Salt and pepper, to taste
1/2 cup dairy sour cream
1 egg beaten with 2 tablespoons milk

Butter Pastry:
3 cups all-purpose flour
1 cup butter, chilled, cut into pieces
1 egg beaten with 1/4 cup water and 1 tablespoon lemon juice

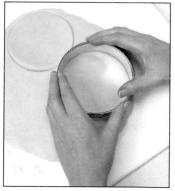

Prepare pastry: Process flour and butter in a food processor until the mixture resembles coarse crumbs. Add egg mixture to flour mixture.

Mix with a fork into a ball; adding more water if needed. Wrap and refrigerate 30 minutes. Preheat oven to 400F (205C). Cook bacon until crisp in a heavy skillet; drain. Add beef and onion. Cook 3 to 4 minutes. Add mushrooms and cook until liquids are absorbed. Stir in tomato paste, thyme, salt, pepper and sour cream and cool. Roll out pastry to 1/4 inch thick. Cut out 4-inch rounds. Spoon a rounded tablespoonful of filling onto each round.

Fold pastry over filling and seal. Place on an ungreased baking sheet. With a fork, press edges together and pierce tops. Brush with egg mixture. Bake 12 to 15 minutes or until golden-brown. Serve hot or cool.

Makes about 48.

— POPCORN PARTY SNACK MIX —

1/4 cup butter or margarine
1/2 teaspoon garlic salt
1/2 teaspoon onion salt
1/4 teaspoon celery salt
1/8 teaspoon cayenne (red) pepper
1-1/2 tablespoons Worcestershire sauce
2 quarts popped popcorn
1-1/2 cups salted mixed nuts
1 cup pretzel sticks

Preheat oven to 275F (135C). Melt butter in small pan. Add garlic, onion salt, celery salt and cayenne. Mix in Worcestershire sauce.

Combine popped corn, nuts and pretzel sticks in a large, shallow baking pan. Add the seasoning mix and toss to mix well. Bake 1 hour, stirring several times.

Makes about 2-1/2 quarts.

SMOKED SALMON PÂTÉ

1 cup smoked red salmon, skinned, boned
   and flaked
1/4 cup mayonnaise
2 tablespoons finely chopped green onion
Fresh herbs for garnish
Crackers, thinly sliced French bread or toasted rye triangles

Combine fish, mayonnaise and onion in
a food processor. Process until smooth.

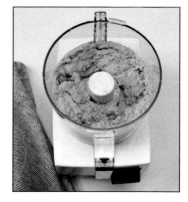

Turn into a small bowl or pot. Garnish
with fresh herbs. Place onto a larger
plate or tray and surround with crackers, bread or toast.

Makes about 12 servings.

– SPICY BAKED CHICKEN WINGS –

2 pounds chicken wings, cut in pieces
1/3 cup cream sherry
1/4 cup soy sauce
1/4 cup plus 2 teaspoons water
1 teaspoon sugar
1/4 teaspoon red (cayenne) pepper
1 garlic clove, peeled and bruised
1 slice fresh gingerroot, 1/8 inch thick
2 teaspoons cornstarch
1/2 teaspoon sesame oil
1 tablespoon Dijon-style mustard

Preheat oven to 300F (150C). Arrange chicken wings in a shallow 3-quart casserole dish.

Combine sherry, soy sauce, 1/4 cup water, sugar, pepper, garlic and ginger-root in a small saucepan; bring to a boil. Pour over chicken wings. Bake, uncovered, 45 minutes.

Drain juices from chicken wings into a small saucepan. Blend cornstarch, 2 teaspoons water, sesame oil and mustard in a small bowl. Stir into chicken juices in saucepan. Bring to a boil. Cook, stirring constantly, until thickened. Pour over wings. Serve wings hot or at room temperature.

Makes about 12 servings.

SPINACH & CORN DIP

1 (8-oz.) package frozen chopped spinach,
  thawed
1 (8-oz.) package frozen whole-kernel corn
1 cup dairy sour cream
1 cup mayonnaise
1 cup water chestnuts, minced
1/2 cup thinly sliced green onion tops
1 to 2 teaspoons seasoned salt
1 teaspoon seasoned pepper
2 unsliced round loaves of rye bread

Squeeze spinach dry. Combine with corn, sour cream, mayonnaise, water chestnuts, onion tops, salt and pepper.

Cover and refrigerate 2 hours or overnight for flavors to blend. Cut a "lid" off the top of one loaf of bread. Carefully scoop out center leaving a 1-inch-thick shell. Cut bread from center and the remaining loaf of bread into small cubes.

Fill bread shell with spinach mixture. Surround with bread cubes. To serve, spread or dip cubes with the spinach-corn filling.

Makes 16 to 20 servings.

— WILD RICE & CHEESE LOG —

1 cup cooked wild rice
1 (8-oz.) package cream cheese, room
   temperature
1 cup (4 oz.) shredded sharp Cheddar cheese
1/2 cup each pitted ripe and green stuffed
   olives, chopped
2 tablespoons instant minced onion
1 cup walnuts, finely chopped
2 teaspoons coarsely ground pepper

Combine 1/2 cup of the wild rice, the
cream cheese, Cheddar cheese, olives
and onion in a large bowl and mix well.
Divide mixture into two parts. Shape
each part into a log about 2 inches in
diameter.

Cut 2 (14-inch) pieces of plastic wrap.
Sprinkle one piece with half of the
remaining wild rice, half the walnuts
and half the black pepper. Place roll on
the mixture, turn and press nuts, rice
and pepper onto all sides to coat. Wrap
tightly and refrigerate until firm.
Repeat with second cheese log. To
serve, unwrap and slice. Serve with
crackers, melba toast or thinly sliced
French bread.

Makes 2 (10-inch) long rolls.

WILD RICE STUFFED MUSHROOMS

12 large white mushrooms
2 tablespoons butter or margarine
2 garlic cloves, minced
1/2 cup cooked wild rice
1/2 cup whipping cream
Salt and freshly ground pepper
1/4 cup freshly grated Parmesan cheese
Fresh rosemary leaves

Preheat oven to 400F (205C). Butter a shallow baking dish. Snap stems off mushrooms and chop. Place caps with tops down in buttered dish.

Melt butter in a medium-size skillet. Add garlic and mushroom stems. Cook over medium heat, stirring, 3 minutes. Add wild rice, cream, salt and pepper and boil 1 minute, stirring, until mixture is thickened.

Spoon wild rice mixture into the mushroom caps. Sprinkle with the Parmesan cheese. Top each mushroom with two or three leaves of rosemary. Bake 10 to 15 minutes or until hot. Serve warm.

Makes 12 appetizers.

Hint
Cover stuffed mushrooms and refrigerate until ready to serve. Bake in a preheated oven until heated through.

BROILED BRIE

1 (1-lb.) wheel Wisconsin Brie
1/2 cup honey
1/2 cup roasted salted sunflower kernels
Wheat crackers or thin French bread slices,
    to serve
Fresh fruit, to serve

Preheat broiler. Unwrap brie and place on an ovenproof plate. Spread top of brie with honey and sprinkle with sunflower kernels.

Just before serving, broil 4 inches from heat until honey is bubbly and sunflower kernels are lightly browned. Serve with crackers or French bread and fruit.

Makes about 16 appetizer servings, 1 ounce cheese per serving.

– WISCONSIN BEER-CHEESE SOUP –

3 tablespoons butter or margarine
1 large onion, chopped
1 celery stalk, chopped
2 medium-size carrots, chopped
3 tablespoons all-purpose flour
2 cups beef broth
2 medium-size potatoes, peeled and cubed
1 (12-oz.) bottle dark beer
1 cup whipping cream
Freshly grated nutmeg
1/8 teaspoon cayenne (red) pepper
Salt
3 cups (12 oz.) shredded sharp
   Cheddar cheese
Additional shredded cheese, to garnish

Melt butter in a large pot. Add onion, celery and carrots; cook until soft, about 5 minutes. Stir in flour; cook 1 minute, stirring. Stir in broth. Add potatoes and beer. Bring to a boil. Reduce heat, cover and simmer 20 minutes or until potatoes are soft.

Transfer vegetables to a food processor or blender. Process until pureed. Return to pan; add cream, nutmeg, cayenne and salt to taste. Reheat to a simmer. Add cheese, 1/2 cup at a time, and stir until melted. Do not boil. Serve hot. Garnish with cheese.

Makes 6 to 8 servings.

BROCCOLI SOUP

3 cups fresh broccoli flowerets with stems
2 tablespoons butter or margarine
1 medium-size onion, minced
2 tablespoons all-purpose flour
2 cups milk
1 teaspoon seasoned salt
1/4 teaspoon pepper
1/2 cup whipping cream
Broccoli flowers for garnish (optional)

Bring broccoli and enough water to cover to a boil in a saucepan. Reduce heat. Cook 5 minutes or until broccoli is tender. Drain. Process broccoli in a food processor until finely chopped.

Melt butter in a medium-size saucepan; add onion and cook 3 minutes or until onion is tender. Stir in flour. Slowly stir in milk. Cook, stirring constantly, until thickened.

Add broccoli, seasoned salt and pepper to flour mixture. Heat to serving temperature. Whisk in cream. Garnish with broccoli flowers, if desired.

Makes 6 to 8 servings.

Variation
Add 1 cup cooked wild rice with chopped broccoli.

–WILD RICE & MUSHROOM SOUP–

2/3 cup wild rice
2-1/2 cups water
2 tablespoons butter or vegetable oil
1 small onion, chopped
1 celery stalk, chopped
1 small carrot, diced
8 ounces mushrooms, sliced
5 cups chicken broth
1 teaspoon dried leaf thyme
1/2 teaspoon rosemary leaves
2 tablespoons dry sherry
Salt and pepper to taste

Wash wild rice in 3 changes of hot tap water until clean. Turn into a large saucepan and add water. Cook, covered, over low heat 40 minutes or until rice is tender. Drain off any excess liquid. Melt butter in a 3- to 4-quart heavy pan. Add onion, celery, carrot and mushrooms. Cook over medium heat until vegetables are tender.

Add wild rice, chicken broth, thyme and rosemary. Bring to a boil. Add sherry. Season with salt and pepper. Serve hot.

Makes 6 servings.

Variation
Reduce chicken stock by 1 cup. Blend 1/2 cup of the chicken stock with 1/4 cup all-purpose flour. Add to remaining soup and cook, stirring, until thickened. Add 1 cup half and half with sherry.

DILLED SALMON SOUP

3 medium-size potatoes, peeled and cubed
3 cups water
3 green onions, cut into 1/2-inch pieces
1 bay leaf
12 ounces boneless salmon fillets or steaks, cubed
1 cup half and half or milk
2 tablespoons all-purpose flour
1 tablespoon butter or margarine
1 teaspoon salt
1/4 teaspoon pepper
2 tablespoons chopped fresh dill or 2 teaspoons dried dill weed

Combine potatoes, water, onions and bay leaf in a large saucepan. Bring to a boil. Reduce heat, cover and simmer 20 minutes or until potatoes are tender. Add fish.

Cover and simmer 5 minutes. Discard bay leaf. Blend half and half and flour in a small bowl; add to soup slowly, stirring. Cover and simmer, stirring occasionally, 5 minutes or until soup thickens and fish is done. Add butter, salt, pepper and dill.

Makes 4 servings.

– Hearty Cabbage Beef Soup –

1/2 small cabbage head, shredded
1 large onion, chopped
5-1/2 cups canned tomato juice
2 cups beef broth
2 tablespoons molasses
2 tablespoons Worcestershire sauce
2 teaspoons salt
1 bay leaf
3 whole black peppercorns
4 whole allspice berries
1 pound lean ground beef
2 tablespoons dried dill weed
1/8 teaspoon garlic powder

Combine cabbage, onion, tomato juice and beef broth. Bring to a boil.

Add molasses, Worcestershire sauce, salt, bay leaf, peppercorns and allspice. Crumble in ground beef, dill and garlic powder. Simmer 1 hour, stirring occasionally. Serve hot.

Makes 6 to 8 servings.

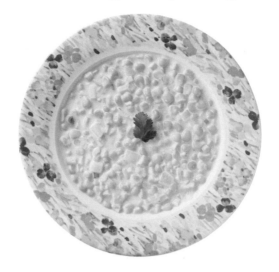

Iowa Corn Chowder

4 bacon slices, diced
2 cups chopped onions
2 tablespoons all-purpose flour
4 cups chicken broth
2 large potatoes, cut into 1/4-inch pieces
1 cup half and half
4 cups whole-kernel corn, fresh or frozen
3 green onions, thinly sliced
Salt and pepper
Chopped fresh cilantro for garnish

Cook bacon in a 3- or 4-quart saucepan over medium heat 5 minutes or until crisp. Remove and reserve bacon.

Add onions to bacon drippings and cook over low heat 10 minutes or until soft. Stir in flour and cook, stirring, 5 minutes.

Add chicken broth and potatoes. Cook over medium heat until potatoes are tender. Add half and half, corn and green onions and cook 10 minutes or until hot. Season with salt and pepper. Add cilantro for garnish. Serve hot.

Makes 6 servings.

— Summer Vegetable Soup —

1 large cauliflower, broken into flowerets
12 ounces baby carrots
12 ounces small new potatoes, quartered
4 ounces small white onions
1 teaspoon salt
4 cups chicken broth or water
4 ounces fresh edible pea pods or snow peas
1-1/2 cups fresh green peas
2 ounces small fresh green beans
2 cups half and half
2 tablespoons all-purpose flour
1 teaspoon sugar
1/8 teaspoon freshly ground white pepper
Shredded fresh spinach leaves for garnish

Combine cauliflower, carrots, potatoes, onions and salt in a large pot. Add broth or water to cover. Bring to a boil over high heat. Reduce heat, cover and simmer 15 minutes or just until vegetables are tender. Add pea pods, peas, green beans (cut into 1-inch pieces if beans are longer than 2 inches) and 1 cup of the half and half to the pot. Simmer 3 minutes.

Combine remaining 1 cup half and half with flour until smooth in a small bowl. Stir into simmering soup and cook, stirring occasionally, until thickened. Add sugar and pepper to soup. Ladle soup into bowls and garnish with fresh spinach leaves.

Makes 6 to 8 servings.

SWEDISH PEA SOUP

**2 cups dried whole yellow Swedish peas or
  yellow split peas
3 quarts water
1 (1-1/2-lb.) smoked ham hock
3 medium-size onions, sliced
1/2 teaspoon ground ginger
1/4 teaspoon whole allspice berries
1 teaspoon dried leaf marjoram
Salt and pepper to taste
Chopped fresh parsley to garnish**

In a large pan, combine peas and water.
Soak overnight. Drain.

Add water and ham hock to peas. Bring
to a boil. Skim off pea shells and fat that
float to top of water. Add onions, ginger and allspice. Simmer 4 to 5 hours
over low heat or until peas are tender.

Remove ham hock, dice meat and discard fat and bone. Return meat to soup.
Season with salt and pepper. Garnish
with chopped parsley and serve.

Makes 6 to 8 servings.

Chicken in Herb Sauce

1/4 cup chopped fresh cilantro
1/4 cup finely chopped drained capers
1 (2-oz.) tin anchovy fillets, chopped
2 tablespoons finely chopped onion
2 tablespoons fresh lemon juice
2 garlic cloves, finely chopped
1 teaspoon Dijon-style mustard
1/2 cup extra-virgin olive oil
2 cups chicken broth
1-1/2 pounds boneless, skinless
   chicken breasts

Combine cilantro, capers, anchovies, onion, lemon juice, garlic and mustard in a small bowl.

Whisk in olive oil. Cover and let stand at room temperature 1 hour, or refrigerate up to 1 week. Bring chicken broth to a simmer in a saucepan. Add chicken breasts, cover and simmer about 5 minutes, turning once, or until chicken is just cooked through.

Drain chicken and cut into thin crosswise slices. Discard broth. Whisk sauce. Arrange chicken on plates, drizzle with sauce and serve.

Makes 6 servings.

– CURRIED CRANBERRY CHICKEN –

4 boneless, skinless chicken breast halves
1 cup whole-berry cranberry sauce
1/2 cup chopped apples
1/2 cup raisins
1/4 cup walnuts, coarsely chopped
2 teaspoons curry powder
1 teaspoon salt
Belgian endive leaves for garnish

Preheat oven to 350F (175C). Butter a shallow baking dish. Arrange chicken breasts in buttered dish. Bake chicken 30 minutes.

Combine cranberry sauce, apples, raisins, walnuts, curry powder and salt in a medium-size bowl.

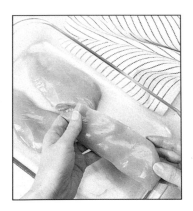

Spread fruit mixture over top of chicken; return to oven and bake 30 minutes longer. Serve hot. Garnish with endive.

Makes 4 servings.

CHICKEN HOT DISH

1 (3-lb.) chicken, cut up
1 large red onion
1 pound small red potatoes
8 ounces baby carrots
4 ounces whole, small mushrooms
4 whole large garlic cloves, peeled
1/4 cup extra-virgin olive oil
1 teaspoon coarse salt
1 teaspoon rosemary leaves
Freshly ground pepper
Fresh rosemary for garnish

Preheat oven to 375F (190C). Arrange chicken pieces in a 13" × 9" baking pan. Cut onion from top to bottom into 1/2-inch wedges. Tuck onion, potatoes, carrots, mushrooms and garlic around the chicken in the pan.

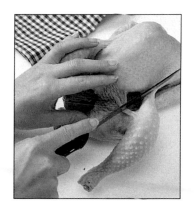

Drizzle olive oil evenly over the vegetables and chicken. Sprinkle with salt, rosemary and pepper. Spray vegetables and chicken with nonstick cooking spray. Bake 1 hour or until chicken pieces are no longer pink in centers and vegetables are tender. Serve hot. Garnish with fresh rosemary.

Makes 4 to 6 servings.

BARBECUED TURKEY LEGS

2 pounds fresh turkey legs or thighs
1/4 cup ketchup
3 tablespoons chili sauce
1 tablespoon brown sugar
1 tablespoon chopped onion
2 teaspoons butter or margarine
2 teaspoons Worcestershire sauce
2 teaspoons prepared mustard
1/2 teaspoon celery seeds
1 garlic clove, minced
Dash hot pepper sauce

Preheat oven to 350F (175C). Wrap turkey in heavy-duty foil.

Place turkey on a baking pan and bake 1-1/2 hours. Turn turkey packets over halfway through baking. Meanwhile, combine remaining ingredients in a small saucepan. Bring to a boil, reduce heat and simmer sauce 10 minutes.

Preheat charcoal grill. Remove turkey from foil. Brush with sauce. Place over charcoal and grill 10 minutes, brushing with sauce and turning occasionally, or until glazed. Serve with remaining sauce. Garnish as desired.

Makes 4 servings.

TURKEY IN PASTRY

1 tablespoon butter or margarine
4 (4- to 5-oz.) turkey breast tenderloins
1 cup cooked wild rice
1/2 cup chopped pecans, toasted
1/4 cup soft bread crumbs
1/4 cup dried currants
1 (17-1/4-oz.) package frozen puff
    pastry, thawed
1 egg, beaten
1-1/4 cups half and half
1 tablespoon cornstarch
1/2 teaspoon each dill weed and dried
    leaf basil
Salt and pepper

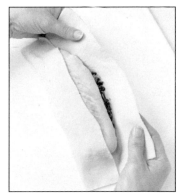

Preheat oven to 375F (190C). Melt butter in a heavy skillet. Add turkey and cook over medium-high heat 5 minutes, turning, or until browned. Combine rice, pecans, bread crumbs and currants in a small bowl. Roll out each pastry sheet to a 17" × 12" rectangle. Cut pastry sheets in halves. Spoon 1/4 of the rice mixture onto the center of each pastry piece. Top each with a turkey tenderloin.

Wrap pastry over turkey, stretching pastry gently. Pinch edges together to seal. Trim ends and seal. Roll trimmings out, cut into strips and arrange on pastry to decorate. Brush with beaten egg. Bake 20 to 25 minutes, until pastry is browned.

Meanwhile, combine half and half, cornstarch, dill weed and basil in a small saucepan. Bring to a boil; cook until thickened, stirring constantly. Add salt and pepper. Serve sauce with turkey pastries.

Makes 4 servings.

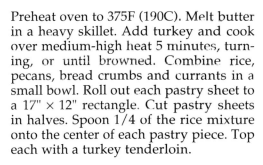

— TURKEY WITH HONEY GLAZE —

4 (4- or 5-oz.) turkey breast tenderloins
2 tablespoons brandy
1/2 cup fresh orange juice
1 tablespoon honey
1-1/2 teaspoons fresh lemon juice
1 tablespoon butter or margarine
Fresh sage leaves and orange slices
   for garnish

Spray a heavy nonstick skillet with non-stick cooking spray. Add turkey and cook over medium-high heat, turning often, until browned on all sides.

Heat brandy in large spoon or small, metal measuring cup. Ignite and pour over the turkey breasts. Remove turkey and slice thinly on the diagonal. Arrange on a heated platter.

Combine orange juice, honey and lemon juice in skillet in which turkey was cooked. Cook over medium heat, stirring constantly, until pan brownings are incorporated and sauce has a syrupy consistency. Whisk in the butter. Spoon sauce over the turkey and garnish with sage leaves and orange slices. Serve immediately.

Makes 4 servings.

Partridge with Tarragon

2 tablespoons butter or margarine
4 partridge breast halves, boned and skinned
1/2 cup dry white wine
1/4 cup sliced green onion
1 (1-lb.) can pear halves in light syrup
1/2 cup half and half or milk
2 teaspoons cornstarch
1/2 teaspoon chopped tarragon leaves
Salt and pepper
Tarragon leaves for garnish

Melt butter in a heavy nonstick skillet. Add partridge; brown over medium-high heat 2 to 3 minutes.

Add wine, green onion and juice from pear halves. Cook over medium heat 10 minutes or until partridge is tender. Remove partridge from pan and keep warm. Boil pan juices down until reduced to 1/2 cup. Blend half and half with cornstarch in a small bowl. Stir into pan juices with tarragon, salt and pepper. Bring to a boil, and cook, stirring, until thickened and smooth.

Return partridge breasts to the sauce; add pear halves and heat to serving temperature. Arrange on a serving platter and spoon sauce over partridge. Garnish with tarragon leaves.

Makes 4 servings.

Variation
Prepare pear fans by cutting even parallel slices from large end of pear to the middle, then press gently to fan.

— Pheasant Baked in Cream —

1 (2- to 3-lb.) pheasant, skinned and cut up
2 tablespoons all-purpose flour
Salt and pepper
1/2 cup dry white wine
1 onion, sliced into rings
4 ounces fresh mushrooms, sliced
2 tablespoons celery leaves, chopped
2 tablespoons chopped parsley
1 teaspoon dried leaf thyme
1 cup half and half

Preheat oven to 350F (175C). Coat pheasant pieces with flour and sprinkle with salt and pepper.

Arrange in a single layer in a 13" × 9" casserole dish. Pour wine over pheasant. Spread the onion rings and sliced mushrooms evenly on top. Sprinkle with celery leaves, parsley and thyme. Pour half and half over pheasant and vegetables.

Cover and bake 1 hour or until pheasant is tender. Pour pan juices into a shallow pan or skillet. Bring to a boil and cook until thickened. Serve pheasant with sauce. Garnish with fresh thyme and celery leaves, if desired.

Makes 6 servings.

ROASTED WILD DUCK

2 wild ducks (about 3 lbs. each), ready to cook
1/2 cup flour seasoned with salt and pepper
1 large onion, quartered
6 bacon slices
1 cup dry red wine
4 garlic cloves, minced or pressed
8 juniper berries
1 teaspoon each dried leaf basil and oregano
2 cups chicken broth
1/4 cup dry white wine
2 tablespoons cornstarch
1/4 cup red currant jelly
2 teaspoons Dijon-style mustard
Sliced oranges and basil for garnish

Rinse and pat ducks dry with paper towels. Preheat oven to 350F (175C). Rub ducks with seasoned flour. Stuff cavity with an onion quarter. Tie legs together.

Place ducks in a Dutch oven. Arrange 3 bacon slices over each duck. Pour red wine into pan. Add garlic, juniper berries, basil and oregano. Fit a piece of waxed paper over ducks, tucking it around the edge of pan. Cover and bake 2-1/2 hours or until tender.

Remove ducks to a heated platter. Add chicken broth to pan; bring to a boil, stirring. Blend white wine with cornstarch in a small bowl, and stir into broth with jelly and mustard. Cook until thickened, stirring. Strain sauce over ducks to glaze; garnish with sliced oranges and parsley. Serve hot.

Makes 4 servings.

RABBIT PIE

1 (3- to 4-lb.) rabbit, cut up
1 small onion, chopped
1 teaspoon rosemary leaves
1 teaspoon salt
1/8 teaspoon freshly ground pepper
2 cups chicken broth
1/4 cup all-purpose flour
1/4 cup dry sherry
1 cup half and half
1 unbaked flat pie crust for 9-inch pie, home-
    made or purchased

Preheat oven to 350F (175C). Arrange rabbit in a shallow 3-quart baking dish.

Sprinkle with onion, rosemary, salt and pepper. Add broth. Cover and bake 1 to 1-1/2 hours or until rabbit is tender. Remove bones from rabbit. Strain broth; measure and add water to make 2 cups. Pour into a saucepan; bring to a boil. Blend flour and sherry until smooth. Whisk into the broth. Cook, stirring, until thickened and smooth. Add half and half.

Put meat from rabbit into deep pie dish or casserole dish. Pour sauce over meat. Fit pastry over the top of pie. Press edges of crust to edge of dish. With tip of a knife, make slashes in the top of the pie. Bake 15 to 20 minutes or until crust is browned.

Makes 6 servings.

— STUFFED BEEF TENDERLOIN —

1 (10-oz.) package fresh spinach, stemmed
1/2 cup (2 oz.) shredded Muenster cheese
1/4 cup dried cranberries
1 egg
3 garlic cloves, minced
2 tablespoons balsamic vinegar
1 teaspoon salt
1/2 teaspoon freshly ground pepper
1 (3-lb.) beef tenderloin, butterflied
1 teaspoon each seasoned salt and pepper
1/3 cup dry red wine

Preheat oven to 425F (220C). Put spinach into a large pan. Cook, covered, over medium heat 5 minutes or until spinach is wilted. Chop and turn into a strainer; squeeze out extra moisture. Combine spinach, cheese, cranberries, egg, garlic, vinegar, salt and pepper.

Flatten tenderloin and spoon filling down the center of the meat. Bring the long sides of the meat up over the filling. Tie with butcher's twine at about 1-inch intervals.

Place in a shallow roasting pan and rub with seasoned salt and seasoned pepper. Pour wine into pan. Bake, uncovered, 10 minutes; reduce the heat to 350F (175C) and bake 20 minutes longer for rare (135 to 140F, 55 to 60C on meat thermometer) or 35 minutes for medium rare (150F, 65C on meat thermometer). Remove from oven and let rest 15 minutes before slicing. Or, after cooling, cover tightly, refrigerate and serve at room temperature.

Makes 10 to 12 servings.

– BEEF & CABBAGE FILLED BUNS –

2 (1/4-oz.) packages active dry yeast
3 tablespoons sugar
1/2 cup warm water (115F, 45C)
1 teaspoon salt
1 cup milk, scalded and cooled to lukewarm
1/2 cup butter, melted and cooled
3 eggs, slightly beaten
5 cups all-purpose flour

Beef Filling:
1 pound extra-lean ground beef
4 cups shredded cabbage
1/3 cup finely chopped onion
1/2 teaspoon caraway seeds
Salt and pepper

Dissolve yeast and sugar in warm water; let stand 5 minutes or until mixture is foamy.

Stir in remaining ingredients to make a moderately stiff dough. Cover and refrigerate 2 hours or overnight.

Preheat oven to 375F (190C). Prepare filling: Cook beef in a large skillet until browned, stirring to break up meat; add cabbage, onion, caraway seeds, salt and pepper. Cover and simmer 15 minutes or until cabbage is soft. Cool.

Roll out yeast dough to form a 20" × 15" rectangle. Using a pastry cutter or knife, cut out 5-inch circles of dough.

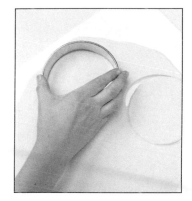

Spoon about 2 tablespoons beef mixture onto the center of each circle. Bring sides to center and pinch dough to seal. Place with seam-side down on a greased baking sheet.

Cover and let rise in a warm place 45 minutes until doubled. Bake 18 to 20 minutes, until golden-brown.

Makes about 18 buns.

— BEEF & VEGETABLE PASTIES —

1-1/4 cups boiling water
1 cup vegetable shortening
1 teaspoon salt
4-1/2 cups all-purpose flour

Filling:
1-1/2 pounds beef round, in 1/2-inch pieces
4 cups diced potatoes
1-1/2 cups diced carrots
1 cup finely chopped onion
2 teaspoons salt
1 teaspoon each dried thyme and rosemary
1/2 teaspoon freshly ground pepper

Combine water, shortening and salt in large bowl; stir until shortening melts. Add flour and stir until stiff dough forms. Gather into a ball. Cover with plastic wrap and refrigerate 1 hour.

Preheat oven to 350F (175C). Divide pastry into 8 parts. On floured board, roll each part out to make a 9-inch circle. In a large bowl, combine all filling ingredients. Place 1 heaping cupful of filling onto center of each pastry round. Brush border with water.

Gently lift dough border up to enclose filling. Pinch a 1/2-inch seam, standing upright across the center of the top of the pasty to make an oval-shaped pie. Pinch seam to flute. Place on an ungreased baking sheet. Repeat with remaining pasties. Bake 1 hour or until golden-brown. Serve warm.

Makes 8 servings.

— Dilled Swedish Meatballs —

1 pound extra-lean ground beef
1 pound ground pork
1/2 cup soft bread crumbs
1/2 cup milk
2 eggs
1/4 cup finely minced onion
1-1/2 teaspoons salt
1/2 teaspoon pepper
1/2 teaspoon ground allspice

Dill Sauce:
2 cups chicken broth
1/4 cup all-purpose flour
1-2/3 cups half and half
2 tablespoons chopped fresh dill
Dill sprigs for garnish

Preheat oven to 450F (230C). Cover a jellyroll pan with foil. Combine meat, crumbs, milk, eggs, onion, salt, pepper and allspice in a large bowl. Beat with an electric mixer until well blended. Shape into 1-inch meatballs. Arrange meatballs in a single layer in the foil-covered pan. Bake 10 minutes, until meatballs are browned and cooked through.

Pour drippings from pan into skillet. Whisk in a little of the broth and flour until mixture is smooth. Whisk in remaining broth. Bring to a boil and gradually add half and half. Cook 2 minutes, stirring, until thickened. Add meatballs to skillet; simmer 10 minutes, stirring occasionally. Sprinkle with dill.

Makes 6 servings.

HOT & SPICY SPARERIBS

3 pounds lean pork spareribs, cut into
    single ribs
1/4 cup butter or margarine
2 cups packed brown sugar
1/2 cup fresh lemon juice
1/4 cup soy sauce
2 garlic cloves, minced
1 teaspoon hot pepper sauce

Place ribs into a large pot; cover with
water. Bring to a boil. Reduce heat and
simmer 30 minutes; skim off foam.
Drain and lift ribs onto paper towels to
drain. Preheat oven to 325F (165C).
Combine butter, brown sugar, lemon
juice, soy sauce, garlic and hot sauce in
a large skillet. Cook, stirring, until
sugar is dissolved, 3 to 5 minutes.

Place ribs in a shallow baking pan.
Cover with sauce. Cover and bake 2
hours, basting occasionally, or until ribs
are tender and glazed. Garnish as
desired.

Makes 4 or 5 main-dish servings or 12
appetizer servings.

—— Midwestern Meat Loaf ——

1 medium-size onion, thinly sliced
1/4 cup fresh parsley
2 pounds extra-lean ground beef
1 (1-lb.) can whole tomatoes
2 eggs
2 bread slices, broken into pieces
1-1/2 teaspoons salt
1-1/2 teaspoons mustard powder
1 teaspoon chili powder
1/2 teaspoon freshly ground pepper

Preheat oven to 350F (175C). Thinly slice onion. Finely chop parsley. Combine all ingredients in a large mixer bowl. Mix until well blended.

Pack into a 9" × 5" loaf pan. Bake 1-1/2 hours or until loaf is browned on top and cooked through. Serve warm or cool in pan. Cut into slices to serve.

Makes 8 servings.

— MUSTARD-TOPPED HAM LOAF —

8 ounces each ground ham, extra-lean ground
    beef and ground lean pork
1/2 cup milk
1/2 cup soft bread crumbs
1 egg, beaten
1 small green bell pepper, finely diced
2 green onions, sliced
1/2 teaspoon salt

Mustard Topping:
2 tablespoons Dijon-style mustard
1/4 cup fine bread crumbs
1/4 cup packed brown sugar

Preheat oven to 375F (190C). Mix ham,
beef, pork, milk, bread crumbs, egg, bell
pepper, onions and salt in a large bowl
until well blended. Shape meat mixture
into a rounded loaf on an ungreased
baking pan.

Spread top of loaf with mustard.
Combine bread crumbs and brown
sugar and pat evenly over loaf. Bake 1
hour, until loaf is firm.

Makes 6 to 8 servings.

— WINE-BRAISED LAMB SHANKS —

4 (1-lb.) lamb shanks
Salt and pepper
About 1 cup all-purpose flour
1 tablespoon olive oil
2 cups dry white wine or water
2 cups chopped fresh tomatoes
2 garlic cloves, minced
2 teaspoons salt
1 teaspoon each dried leaf thyme, basil
    and oregano
1 tablespoon chopped fresh parsley
Buttered noodles, wild rice or wheat pilaf

Preheat oven to 350F (175C). Sprinkle lamb shanks with salt and pepper and roll in flour. Heat oil in a heavy Dutch oven. Add lamb and brown over medium heat on all sides.

Add wine, garlic, the 2 teaspoons salt, thyme, basil, oregano and parsley. Cover and bake 2 hours or until meat is very tender. Serve 1 lamb shank per person over cooked, buttered noodles, wild rice or wheat pilaf. Spoon drippings over each serving. Garnish with fresh thyme, if desired.

Makes 4 servings.

— PORK & RASPBERRY SAUCE —

1 (1-1/2-lb.) pork tenderloin
Salt and pepper
1 cup fresh mint leaves or 1/2 cup dried leaf
   mint
2/3 cup water
1/4 cup raspberry vinegar
1/3 cup sugar
2 tablespoons sliced green onion
1 tablespoon cornstarch
1 tablespoon water
1-1/2 cups fresh or frozen raspberries, thawed

Preheat oven to 350F (175C). Rub pork with salt and pepper. Place into a shallow baking pan. Roast 30 minutes or until pork is no longer pink in center.

Combine mint leaves, water, vinegar, sugar and green onion in a saucepan. Bring to a boil. Reduce heat, cover and simmer 15 minutes.

Strain; reserve liquid. Return liquid to saucepan and bring to a boil. Mix cornstarch and water in a small bowl. Stir into boiling liquid. Cook and stir until thickened. Remove from heat. Fold raspberries into sauce. Cut pork tenderloin diagonally into 1/2-inch slices and serve with raspberry sauce.

Makes 6 servings.

— Roasted Pork with Garlic —

1 (3- to 4-lb.) boneless pork loin or shoulder
8 garlic cloves, peeled
2 tablespoons fennel seeds
1 tablespoon each dried leaf thyme, oregano,
    basil, paprika, coarse black pepper and
    coarse salt
1 teaspoon red pepper flakes
1 tablespoon olive oil
Thyme sprigs for garnish

Preheat oven to 350F (175C). Remove strings from pork loin and place on work surface with the inside facing up.

Combine garlic, 1 tablespoon of the fennel seeds and remaining spices in a blender. Process until pulverized. Mix in remaining fennel seeds and rub half the seasoning mixture onto the cut side of meat.

Reroll meat into a log and tie with string at 1-inch intervals. Rub with oil and remaining seasoning mixture. Place roast on a rack in a shallow baking pan. Roast 25 minutes per pound or until pork is no longer pink in center. Let cool 10 minutes before slicing. Garnish with thyme sprigs.

Makes 6 to 8 servings.

SLOW-ROASTED STEW

3 pounds onions, thinly sliced
1-1/2 pounds beef stew meat, cubed
1 pound boneless lean pork, cubed
8 ounces boneless lamb stew meat, cubed
1 tablespoon salt
1 tablespoon whole allspice
1/2 teaspoon whole black peppercorns
1 each red, yellow and green bell peppers,
  diced
Mashed potatoes for serving

Preheat oven to 300F (150C). Spray a heavy Dutch oven with nonstick cooking spray. Alternate layers of onions, meats, salt and spices, beginning and ending with onions. Pack into pan.

Cut a sheet of parchment paper or waxed paper large enough to fit the top of the meat. Press paper firmly onto the meat and tuck around edges between meat and sides of pot. Cover.

Bake 5-1/2 hours. Do not remove cover during this time. Remove stew from oven, remove and discard paper. Add bell peppers to top of stew. Bake 30 minutes longer. Serve with potatoes.

Makes 10 to 12 servings.

Note
There is no liquid added to this stew, but there will be plenty after cooking. It is traditionally never thickened. This is an incredibly simple party dish.

SPICY VENISON CHILI

1 pound dry red beans, picked over
Water
2 pounds coarsely ground venison
1 large onion, finely chopped
3 garlic cloves, finely minced
3 to 4 tablespoons chili powder
1 tablespoon ground cumin
1/8 to 1 teaspoon red pepper flakes
2 (14-1/2-oz.) cans tomatoes
Salt and pepper
Fresh cilantro leaves

Soak beans overnight in enough water to cover by 2 inches.

Drain, add fresh water to cover and boil 10 minutes. Reduce heat, cover and simmer until tender, 1 to 2 hours. Cook venison, onion and garlic until venison is browned, stirring to break up meat. Add chili powder, cumin and red pepper flakes. Add tomatoes, breaking them up with a spoon. Simmer venison and tomatoes 10 minutes.

Add beans with their cooking liquid. Cover and simmer 30 to 40 minutes. Add salt and pepper to taste. Top with cilantro leaves.

Makes 6 to 8 servings.

—— VENISON CABBAGE ROLLS ——

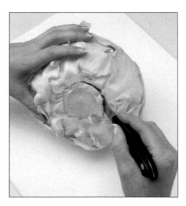

1 large cabbage, about 3 pounds, cored
2 tablespoons butter or margarine
1 small onion, minced
1 pound ground venison
2 cups cooked rice
1 egg, beaten
1 tablespoon whole-grain mustard
1 teaspoon each salt, pepper and dried leaf
   marjoram
1/2 cup pine nuts (optional)
1/4 cup packed brown sugar
2 tablespoons butter or margarine, melted
Marjoram sprigs for garnish

Preheat oven to 325F (165C). Grease a
13" × 9" baking pan. Bring a large pot of
water to a boil. Place cabbage into
water. Boil cabbage, removing 16 outer
leaves as they are tender. Drain well.
Finely chop enough inner leaves to
make 3 cups.

Melt 2 tablespoons butter in a large skillet; add onion and chopped cabbage.
Cook over medium-high heat 10 minutes, stirring, or until vegetables are
tender and liquids have evaporated.
Combine cabbage mixture, venison,
rice, egg, mustard, salt, pepper, marjoram leaves and pine nuts, if using.

Spoon 1/3 cup stuffing into cabbage
leaves and roll up. Place cabbage rolls,
seam-side down, close together in prepared pan. Sprinkle with brown sugar;
drizzle with melted butter. Cover with
foil and bake 1 hour. Remove cover and
bake 20 to 25 minutes or until cabbage
rolls are browned. Garnish with marjoram sprigs, if desired.

Makes 8 servings.

TROUT WITH MUSHROOM SAUCE

2 pounds rainbow trout fillets, 1/2 inch thick
Salt and pepper
3 tablespoons butter or margarine
1 cup sliced fresh mushrooms
1/2 cup sliced celery
1/4 cup thinly sliced green onion
1 tablespoon all-purpose flour
2 tablespoons chopped fresh basil leaves
1/2 teaspoon salt
1 cup half and half
1/2 cup coarsely chopped walnuts
Fresh basil leaves for garnish

Preheat oven to 350F (175C). Butter a 13" × 9" baking pan. Sprinkle fish with salt and pepper and place in pan with skin-side down. Bake 10 minutes.

Melt butter in a medium-size skillet. Add mushrooms, celery and onion; sauté until tender, 5 minutes. Stir in flour, basil and salt. Add half and half; cook until sauce is thickened, stirring constantly.

Pour sauce over fish. Sprinkle with chopped walnuts. Bake 10 minutes longer or until fish just begins to flake when probed with a fork. Garnish with fresh basil leaves.

Makes 4 to 6 servings.

FISH IN BEER BATTER

1 cup all-purpose flour
1 teaspoon each baking powder, salt
   and paprika
1 egg, beaten
1 cup beer
2 pounds smelts or fish fillets cut into
   1/2-inch strips
Vegetable oil for frying
Parsley sprigs for garnish

Combine flour, baking powder, salt and paprika in a medium-size bowl. Stir in egg and beer (add more beer if batter thickens upon standing).

Heat 1 inch of vegetable oil in skillet or electric skillet to 375F (190C) or until a bread cube browns in 1 minute.

Dry fish with paper towels. Dip fish in batter and fry in the oil 2 to 3 minutes until brown and crisp, turning once. Drain on paper towels. Garnish with parsley.

Makes 6 to 8 servings.

- BAKED FISH WITH MUSHROOMS -

1/2 ounce dried morel mushrooms or
   chanterelle mushrooms, crushed
4 (6-oz.) fish fillets
Salt and pepper
3 tablespoons butter or margarine, melted
1 garlic clove, minced
1 teaspoon chopped fresh dill or dried dill
1/4 cup sliced green onion
1 cup whipping cream
1 tablespoon dry sherry
Lemon wedges and fresh dill for garnish

Preheat oven to 350F (175C). Butter a shallow baking dish large enough to hold fish. Place mushrooms in a small bowl; cover with hot water. Let stand 30 minutes. Pat fish dry; sprinkle with salt and pepper. Place in buttered baking dish. Combine butter and the garlic in a small bowl. Brush fish with the garlic butter. Sprinkle with the dill. Bake 10 to 15 minutes, until fish changes from translucent to opaque.

Meanwhile, add green onion, soaked mushrooms with soaking liquid and cream to a medium-size saucepan; simmer until sauce is reduced and thickened, stirring occasionally. Add sherry and salt and pepper to taste. Serve sauce with the baked fish.

Makes 4 servings.

– Salmon with Garlic Butter –

**4 farm-raised salmon fillets, 1-3/4 to 2
  pounds total
Salt and pepper
3 tablespoons butter or margarine
1 garlic clove, minced
3 tablespoons fresh lemon juice
Chopped fresh parsley
Lemons and fresh dill for garnish**

Preheat oven to 350F (175C). Butter a
13" × 9" baking dish. Place salmon fillets
skin-side down in buttered dish.
Sprinkle with salt and pepper.

Heat butter in skillet. Add garlic and
cook 2 minutes until garlic is softened
but not browned. Brush fish with the
mixture. Bake 20 minutes or until fish
just begins to flake.

Sprinkle with chopped fresh parsley.
Cut lemons into wedges; remove seeds.
Serve fish with lemon wedges.

Makes 4 servings.

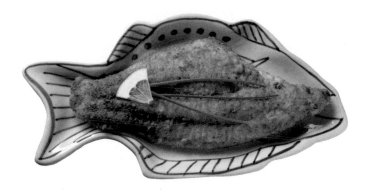

– FISHERMEN'S PAN-FRIED FILLETS –

6 catfish or large walleye fillets
Corn oil for frying
1 cup crushed crackers
1/2 cup rye flour
1/2 teaspoon salt
1/2 teaspoon freshly ground pepper
1 egg, beaten
Lemon wedges for garnish
Fresh chives for garnish

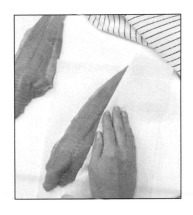

Pat fillets dry with paper towels. Heat a heavy 10-inch skillet and pour in enough oil to cover the bottom by about 1/8 inch. Heat oil over medium-high heat.

Mix cracker crumbs, flour, salt and pepper in a shallow pan. Dip fish into beaten egg, then into crumb mixture, pressing crumbs firmly onto each side.

Pan-fry coated fillets in hot oil 3 minutes on each side or until golden-brown. Garnish with lemon and chives.

Makes 6 servings.

— Fish with Sesame Butter —

2 pounds northern pike, walleye fillets or
  other fillets
1 teaspoon salt
1/2 teaspoon freshly ground pepper
1/2 cup butter or margarine, melted
1/4 cup fresh lemon juice
Dash of Worcestershire sauce
6 tablespoons sesame seeds, toasted
Lemon slices for garnish
Fresh dill or parsley for garnish

Preheat oven to 350F (175C). Butter a
shallow 13" × 9" baking dish. Arrange
fish in the dish, overlapping, if necessary. Sprinkle with salt and pepper;
brush with some of the melted butter.
Bake 20 minutes or until fish just begins
to flake when probed with a fork.

Heat remaining butter until lightly
browned. Add lemon juice, Worcestershire sauce and sesame seeds. Spoon
over baked fish. Garnish with lemon
and dill or parsley.

Makes 4 servings.

POOR MAN'S LOBSTER

2 cups water
1/4 small onion, sliced
1 bay leaf
1/2 cup sliced celery tops
1 cup dry white wine
1 teaspoon salt
2 pounds fresh or frozen cod, perch or white-
**   fish, cut into 2-inch pieces**
1/4 cup butter or margarine
1/4 cup all-purpose flour
1/2 cup half and half or milk
Salt and pepper
Chopped chives for garnish

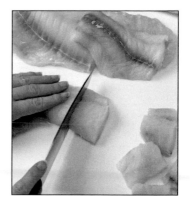

Pour water into a deep skillet and add onion, bay leaf, celery tops, white wine and the 1 teaspoon salt. Bring to a boil, reduce heat and simmer 15 minutes. Add fish to simmering stock. Simmer 12 to 15 minutes or until fish just begins to flake when probed with a fork. Lift fish chunks carefully with slotted spoon onto a heated dish.

Strain stock into a 2-cup measuring cup; measure 2 cups. Melt butter in a saucepan; add flour and whisk over medium heat 1 or 2 minutes or until smooth. Whisk in the stock; bring to a boil and boil until thickened, stirring. Whisk in half and half. Add salt and pepper to taste. Add fish and heat until hot. Top with chopped chives.

Makes 4 to 6 servings.

SALMON LOAF

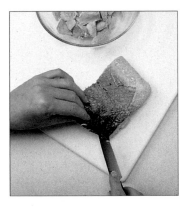

1 (15-1/2-oz.) can salmon, drained, skin and
    bones removed or 1-1/2 cups flaked
    cooked salmon
2 cups soft bread crumbs
1/3 cup finely minced onion
1/4 cup milk
2 eggs, beaten
2 tablespoons minced parsley
1 tablespoon fresh lemon juice
1 teaspoon dill weed

Dilled Meringue: (optional)
1 egg white
1/4 cup mayonnaise
1 teaspoon dill weed

Preheat oven to 350F (175C). Grease a
baking sheet. Combine salmon, bread
crumbs, onion, milk, eggs, parsley,
lemon juice and dill weed.

Shape mixture into a loaf on the pan.
Bake 45 minutes or until loaf is lightly
browned. If desired, prepare meringue:
Beat egg white until stiff but not dry;
fold in the mayonnaise and dill weed.
Spread evenly over the salmon loaf
before baking and bake until meringue
is lightly browned.

Makes 6 servings.

STUFFED LAKE TROUT

1 (4- to 6-lb.) whole Lake Superior Trout or
    whole Coho salmon, ready to cook
1 teaspoon celery salt
1/4 cup extra-virgin olive oil
4 garlic cloves, minced
1/2 cup minced green onions
2 cups soft bread crumbs
4 tablespoons fresh lemon juice
2 tablespoons chopped fresh cilantro
1/2 teaspoon salt
1/2 cup butter or margarine, melted
1/4 cup snipped fresh chives
2 tablespoons fresh lemon juice
Whole chives for garnish

Preheat oven to 400F (205C). Remove
fish head. Rub inside and out with the
celery salt. Heat olive oil in a medium-
size skillet; add garlic and onions and
sauté 3 to 4 minutes until garlic is softened. Combine onion mixture, crumbs,
2 tablespoons of the lemon juice,
cilantro and salt in a medium-size bowl.
Place fish on a piece of foil large
enough to enclose it. Stuff fish with the
crumb mixture. Seal foil.

Bake fish 10 minutes per pound or 40 to
60 minutes. Combine melted butter,
snipped chives and remaining lemon
juice in a small bowl. Serve butter sauce
with fish. Garnish with chives.

Makes 8 to 10 servings.

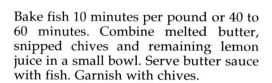

MARINATED CATFISH

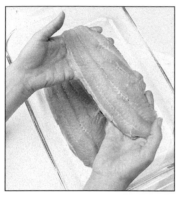

4 catfish fillets, about 1-1/2 pounds total
2 tablespoons red-wine vinegar
1 garlic clove, minced
1 teaspoon Dijon-style mustard
1/4 teaspoon each paprika and dried leaf
    oregano
Dash red (cayenne) pepper
1/4 cup olive oil or corn oil
Salt and pepper
2 tablespoons chopped parsley
Lemon twists for garnish

Pat fish dry with a paper towel. Place in a shallow glass or ceramic baking dish.

Mix vinegar, garlic, mustard, paprika, oregano and cayenne in a small bowl. Beat in oil until blended; pour over fish. Cover and refrigerate 30 minutes.

Preheat broiler. Cover a broiler pan with foil. Remove fish from marinade. Place on foil-covered pan. Sprinkle with salt and pepper. Broil fish 8 to 10 minutes without turning, basting with the marinade often, until golden-brown and cooked through. Sprinkle with parsley and garnish with lemon twists.

Makes 4 to 6 servings.

BRUNCH BAKED EGGS

2 tablespoons butter or margarine
2 tablespoons all-purpose flour
1 cup milk
1/2 teaspoon salt
1/8 teaspoon red pepper flakes
Dash of Worcestershire sauce
1-1/2 cups (6 oz.) shredded sharp Cheddar
    cheese
8 ounces thinly sliced Canadian bacon
2 tomatoes, sliced
8 to 10 eggs
2 tablespoons butter or margarine
1/2 cup fresh bread crumbs

Preheat oven to 325F (165C). Melt butter in a small saucepan and blend in flour. Whisk in milk and bring to a boil, stirring until smooth and thickened. Add salt, pepper flakes and Worcestershire sauce. Mix in 1 cup of the cheese.

Butter a 2-quart casserole dish. Line casserole dish with Canadian bacon. Arrange tomato slices over bacon. Crack eggs, one at a time in a small bowl; pour over tomatoes, being careful not to break yolks. Pour cheese sauce over eggs. Top with remaining 1/2 cup shredded cheese.

Melt butter in a skillet and add bread crumbs; mix until crumbs are coated with butter. Sprinkle crumbs over cheese. Bake 20 minutes or just until eggs are set.

Makes 8 servings.

– CORN, HAM & CHEESE STRATA –

8 slices multi-grain bread, crusts removed
8 ounces sharp Cheddar cheese, cut into
  1/2-inch cubes
1 (9-oz.) package frozen whole-kernel corn
1 cup turkey ham, diced into 1/2-inch pieces
6 eggs, slightly beaten
2 cups half and half or milk
2 tablespoons chopped fresh basil
1/2 teaspoon dry mustard
1/2 teaspoon salt
Basil sprigs for garnish

Butter a 13" × 9" pan. Cut bread into cubes. Spread bread cubes in bottom of buttered pan.

Top with the cheese, corn and ham, distributing evenly. Combine eggs, half and half, basil, mustard and salt. Pour over ingredients in pan. Cover and refrigerate overnight. Remove from refrigerator 1 hour before baking. Preheat oven to 325F (165C). Bake 1-1/2 hours or until puffy and browned.

If desired, prepare Mushroom Sauce: Sauté 1 pound sliced mushrooms in 2 tablespoons butter in a large skillet over medium heat 10 minutes or until tender. Sprinkle 3 tablespoons flour over mushrooms. Mix well; stir in 2 cups half and half. Bring to a boil; cook, stirring, until thickened. Add salt and pepper to taste. Serve hot with baked strata.

Makes 8 servings.

Farmer's Omelet

2 tablespoons butter or margarine
2 cups diced uncooked potatoes
1/4 cup finely chopped onion
1 cup diced ham
1/4 cup chopped fresh parsley
6 eggs
1/2 teaspoon salt
Freshly ground pepper
2 tablespoons milk
1/2 cup (2 oz.) shredded Colby, Cheddar or
    Brick cheese

Melt butter in a 10-inch nonstick skillet. Add potatoes and onion; cover. Cook over medium heat 20 minutes, stirring occasionally to brown evenly, or until potatoes are tender and golden-brown. Add ham; heat through. Sprinkle with parsley.

Beat eggs, salt, pepper and milk together in a medium-size bowl. Pour mixture over potatoes and ham. Cover and cook 10 minutes or until eggs are almost set. With a spatula, lift around edge of pan to allow egg mixture to run under omelet during cooking. Sprinkle with cheese. Cover and cook until cheese melts. Cut into wedges.

Makes 4 to 6 servings.

— MACARONI & FOUR CHEESES —

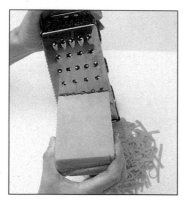

4 cups elbow macaroni
1/4 cup butter or margarine
1/4 cup all-purpose flour
2-1/2 cups milk
1 cup (4 oz.) each shredded Wisconsin
   provolone and Cheddar cheese
1 teaspoon each mustard powder and salt
Freshly ground pepper
1 cup diced Wisconsin mozzarella cheese
1/2 cup freshly grated Wisconsin
   Parmesan cheese
1 teaspoon paprika
Julienned vegetables and parsley for garnish

Cook macaroni according to package directions until al dente. Drain. Preheat oven to 350F (175C). Butter a 2-quart casserole dish. Melt butter in a saucepan; stir in flour. Slowly whisk in milk, and bring to a boil; cook, stirring, until sauce thickens. Add provolone cheese, Cheddar cheese, mustard, salt and pepper. Stir until cheeses melt.

Combine sauce and cooked macaroni. Stir in mozzarella cheese. Turn into buttered dish. Top with Parmesan cheese and sprinkle with paprika. Bake 30 to 40 minutes or until bubbly and top is browned. Cut into squares. Garnish with vegetables and parsley.

Makes 6 servings.

— BAKED NORWEGIAN OMELET —

4 eggs
1/4 cup water
1/2 teaspoon salt
1/2 pound shredded Jarlsberg cheese
1/2 cup diced red bell pepper
1/4 cup minced fresh chives
Red and green bell pepper rings for garnish

Preheat oven to 400F (205C). Butter a shallow 1-1/2-quart baking dish. Whisk together eggs, water and salt in a medium-size bowl.

Pour egg mixture into baking dish. Sprinkle with cheese, bell pepper and chives. Bake 15 to 20 minutes or until eggs are set and cheese is melted. Serve immediately. Garnish with bell pepper.

Makes 3 to 4 servings.

PUFFY OVEN PANCAKE

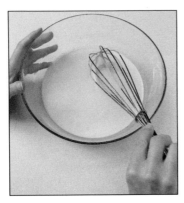

4 eggs
1 cup milk
1 cup all-purpose flour
2 teaspoons sugar
1 teaspoon salt
1/4 cup butter
Powdered sugar
Lemon wedges
Fresh berries or other fruit

Whisk together eggs, milk, flour, sugar and salt in a large bowl until smooth. Cover and let stand 30 minutes.

Preheat oven to 450F (230C). Place butter into a shallow 3-quart round or oval baking dish or a 13" × 9" pan. Place pan into oven until butter is melted. Tip pan to coat bottom and sides with butter.

Pour egg mixture into pan. Bake 15 to 20 minutes or until pancake is puffed and golden. Remove from oven and sift powdered sugar over pancake. Serve immediately. Top individual servings with lemon wedges, fresh fruit or whipped cream.

Makes 4 servings.

Ratatouille with Eggs

1/3 cup extra-virgin olive oil
3 garlic cloves, minced
1 medium-size onion, diced
1 green bell pepper, diced
2 large tomatoes, chopped
4 cups eggplant, peeled and diced
4 cups diced zucchini
3 tablespoons chopped fresh basil or 1 table-
    spoon dried leaf basil
1 teaspoon salt
1/2 teaspoon freshly ground black pepper
8 eggs
1/4 cup freshly grated Parmesan cheese

Heat olive oil in a deep, nonstick wok or casserole dish. Add garlic and onion and stir-fry 2 minutes over high heat. Add bell pepper, tomatoes, eggplant, zucchini, basil, salt and black pepper. Reduce heat to low and stir-fry 6 minutes. Turn into a 13" × 9" baking dish. (Cover and refrigerate until the next day, if desired.)

Preheat oven to 400F (205C). Bake casserole 20 minutes or until very hot. Make 8 indentations in the mixture. Add 1 egg to each. Sprinkle cheese evenly over the top. Bake 10 minutes or until eggs are set.

Makes 8 servings.

SQUAW CORN

6 bacon slices, diced
2 tablespoons minced onion
1/2 green bell pepper, diced
1/2 red bell pepper, diced
1 (1-lb.) package frozen whole-kernel corn
1 teaspoon each dried leaf basil and oregano
1/2 teaspoon each salt and black pepper
4 eggs
4 slices bread, toasted, buttered and cut into
     triangles
Fresh parsley for garnish

Cook bacon in a large skillet until par-
tially cooked. Drain off fat. Add onion
and bell peppers. Cook 1 minute. Add
corn, basil, oregano, salt and black pepper. Heat through.

Make 4 wells in the corn mixture; Crack
eggs, one at a time in a small bowl;
pour into wells, being careful not to
break yolks. Cover and cook until egg
whites are done; turn with a spatula.

Scramble just until mixed; spoon mixture onto toast triangles. Garnish with
parsley.

Makes 4 servings.

GRILLED BRATWURST

8 fresh or smoked, fully cooked bratwurst
1 (12-oz.) bottle beer
2 tablespoons butter
1 large onion, thinly sliced
2 tablespoons brown sugar
2 tablespoons vinegar
1 tablespoon ketchup
1/2 teaspoon salt
8 white or rye buns
Dark whole-grain mustard

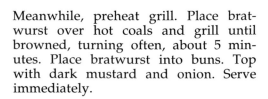

Simmer bratwurst and beer in a wide saucepan 10 minutes or until fresh bratwurst is cooked through. Drain and reserve liquid.

Put butter into a heavy skillet and place over medium-low heat. Add onion and cook, stirring often, until onion is soft and lightly browned, 10 to 15 minutes. Add brown sugar, vinegar, ketchup, salt and bratwurst cooking liquid; bring to a boil and cook until liquid has evaporated and onion is soft and glazed.

Meanwhile, preheat grill. Place bratwurst over hot coals and grill until browned, turning often, about 5 minutes. Place bratwurst into buns. Top with dark mustard and onion. Serve immediately.

Makes 4 servings of 2 bratwurst each, or 8 servings of 1 bratwurst each.

– BARBECUED BEEF SANDWICHES –

1/2 cup cider vinegar
1/2 cup tomato ketchup
3 tablespoons Worcestershire sauce
Few drops of hot pepper sauce
2 tablespoons brown sugar
1 tablespoon mixed pickling spices
1 teaspoon whole-grain mustard
1 teaspoon salt
1 tablespoon corn oil
1 garlic clove, minced
1 (4-1/2-lb.) beef boneless round or brisket
Buttered white or rye sandwich buns
Additional mustard

Preheat oven to 350F (175C). In a 2-quart saucepan, combine all ingredients except meat, buns and additional mustard. Simmer 5 minutes.

Place beef in a 13" × 9" baking dish. Pour sauce over beef. Cover and roast 2-1/2 hours or until meat is tender. Cool 30 minutes.

Slice thinly and return to sauce. Cover and bake 1 hour longer, turning meat in sauce frequently. Spoon beef into buttered buns. Offer mustard on the side.

Makes 16 to 20 servings.

— TURKEY & HAM SANDWICHES —

6 English muffins, halved
6 teaspoons butter
1 pound thinly sliced ham
1 pound thinly sliced turkey
1/2 onion, thinly sliced
2 tomatoes, each cut into 6 slices
2 (10-oz.) packages broccoli, cooked
 and drained

Cheese Sauce:
2 tablespoons butter margarine
2 tablespoons all-purpose flour
2 cups half and half
1-1/2 cups (6 oz.) shredded Cheddar cheese
1/2 teaspoon salt
1/2 teaspoon paprika

Preheat broiler. Arrange muffin halves on a baking sheet and broil halves to toast on 1 side. Spread each half with 1 teaspoon butter. On each muffin half, layer ham, turkey, onion, tomato and a broccoli stalk.

To make Cheese Sauce: In a medium-size saucepan, heat butter until melted. Stir in flour. Whisk in half and half; bring to a boil and cook until thickened, stirring. Stir in cheese, salt and paprika.

Spoon sauce over sandwiches; place under broiler and broil 3 to 4 inches from heat until bubbly.

Makes 12 sandwich halves.

MIDWESTERN HOAGIE

1 loaf (1 lb.) crusty French bread
1/4 cup mayonnaise
2 garlic cloves, minced
8 ounces thinly sliced roasted turkey breast
4 ounces thinly sliced turkey pastrami
4 ounces sliced Swiss cheese or Cheddar
   cheese
3 large tomatoes, sliced
1 (6-oz.) jar marinated artichoke hearts,
   drained
1/2 cup sliced pitted ripe olives
2 large dill pickles, sliced lengthwise
1 mild red or white onion, thinly sliced
Chopped parsley

Cut bread in half horizontally. Hollow out soft bread from top and bottom halves, leaving a 1/2-inch shell. Combine mayonnaise and garlic in a small bowl; spread on the bread. Layer turkey breast, pastrami and cheese on the bottom half of the bread. Top with tomatoes. Slice artichoke hearts and layer over tomatoes. Sprinkle with olives and top with pickles and onion. Sprinkle with parsley.

Place top crust on the filling and press down firmly. Seal tightly in plastic wrap and foil. If made ahead, refrigerate. Just before serving, place the wrapped sandwich on a flat surface, press down firmly and cut into wedges.

Makes 2 to 3 servings.

— SAUSAGE STUFFED RYE BUNS —

1 (1/4-oz.) package active dry yeast
1 cup warm water (105 to 115F, 40 to 45C)
2 tablespoons molasses
2 tablespoons vegetable oil or melted butter
1 cup dark rye flour
2 cups all-purpose flour
2 teaspoons salt
1 pound bulk-style Italian sausage
1 cup sliced green onions
1 (10-oz.) package frozen chopped spinach,
   thawed, squeezed dry
1 cup ricotta cheese
1 egg, beaten

Combine yeast, water, molasses and 1 teaspoon of the salt in a medium-size bowl; let stand 5 minutes. With an electric mixer, beat in oil, rye flour and 1 cup all-purpose flour until smooth. Let stand 15 minutes. Stir in the remaining flour. Knead dough on a floured surface until smooth.

Cover and refrigerate 2 hours or overnight. Cook sausage and green onions in a large skillet until meat is browned; drain off fat. Mix sausage, spinach, ricotta, egg and remaining salt. Preheat oven to 400F (205C). Grease a baking sheet. Remove dough from refrigerator and roll out on floured board to make a 16-inch square. Cut into 4-inch squares.

Place 1/3 cup filling in the center of each square, bring 2 opposite points of the square up over the filling and seal. Place on greased baking sheet. Bake 15 to 20 minutes or until golden. Serve hot or at room temperature.

Makes 16 buns.

SLOPPY JOES

1 pound extra-lean ground beef
1/2 cup chopped onion
1/2 cup chopped green bell pepper
1 teaspoon salt
1 teaspoon chili powder
1/2 teaspoon ground cumin
1/2 teaspoon paprika
1/4 teaspoon pepper
1 cup tomato ketchup
1 cup chopped fresh or canned tomatoes
8 to 10 warmed hamburger buns

Place a large nonstick skillet over medium-high heat. Add beef, onion and bell pepper. Cook until meat is no longer pink, stirring to break up meat.

Add salt, chili powder, cumin, paprika, pepper, ketchup and tomatoes. Simmer 5 minutes. Split the hamburger buns. Spoon meat mixture into buns to serve.

Makes 8 to 10 servings.

– Chicken & Wild Rice Salad –

3 cups cooked wild rice
3 cups cooked diced chicken
1/3 cup finely sliced green onions
1 (8-oz.) can sliced water chestnuts, drained
1/2 teaspoon salt
1/4 teaspoon pepper
2/3 cup mayonnaise
1/3 cup milk
2 tablespoons fresh lemon juice
1/4 teaspoon dried leaf tarragon
1 (8-oz.) can mandarin oranges, drained
1 cup salted cashews
Green onion brushes for garnish

Combine wild rice, chicken, onions, water chestnuts, salt and pepper in a large bowl. Combine mayonnaise, milk, lemon juice and tarragon in a small bowl. Stir into the wild rice mixture until just blended. Refrigerate 2 to 3 hours before serving.

Just before serving, fold in oranges and cashews.

Makes 8 servings.

Note
To make gren onion brushes, cut off green leaves and part of white part of each onion. Insert knife about 2 inches from root end and make a straight cut toward top. Rotate onion slightly; make a second cut 1/8 inch from first and parallel. Repeat.

CREAMY COLESLAW

6 cups shredded white cabbage
3/4 cup shredded carrot
1/2 cup each finely chopped celery, green
   bell pepper, red bell pepper and parsley

Creamy Boiled Dressing:
1/4 cup each cider vinegar and water
2 tablespoons sugar
1 tablespoon all-purpose flour
1 teaspoon each mustard powder and salt
1/2 teaspoon each celery seeds and
   mustard seeds
1/4 cup whipping cream or evaporated milk
2 eggs, beaten

Prepare dressing: Combine vinegar, water, sugar, flour, mustard, salt, celery seeds and mustard seeds in a small saucepan. Bring mixture to a boil, stirring constantly.

Whisk cream and eggs together in a small bowl and whisk in a small amount of the boiling mixture until smooth. Return to saucepan and cook 1 minute longer. Remove from heat, cover and cool.

Combine vegetables in a large salad bowl. Mix in the dressing. Cover and refrigerate 2 to 3 hours before serving.

Makes 6 servings.

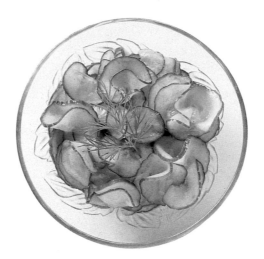

DANISH CUCUMBER SALAD

1 (16-inch) European-style cucumber or 2
   (8-inch) cucumbers
1 cup water
1 cup white vinegar
1 cup sugar
1 teaspoon salt
1/4 teaspoon ground white pepper
Fresh dill sprigs for garnish

Cut cucumbers into paper-thin slices, making about 4 cups of slices.

Combine water, vinegar, sugar, salt and pepper; stir until sugar dissolves. Add cucumbers. Refrigerate 4 to 6 hours. Drain. Serve in a pretty glass bowl. Garnish with fresh dill sprigs.

Makes 6 to 8 servings.

—— GERMAN POTATO SALAD ——

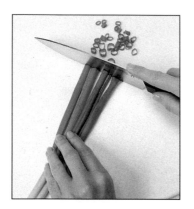

6 medium-size red potatoes, sliced
1 (10-3/4-oz.) can double-strength chicken
  broth
1/2 cup olive oil or vegetable oil
1/4 cup cider vinegar
1/4 cup sugar
1 tablespoon German-style mustard
1 teaspoon salt
2 green onions, thinly sliced
Freshly ground pepper
1 bunch parsley, finely minced

Put potatoes into a medium-size saucepan, cover with water and simmer 15 minutes or until tender. Drain potatoes and turn into a bowl.

Combine chicken broth, oil, vinegar, sugar, mustard, salt and onions in the saucepan and bring to a boil. Pour over the potatoes. Sprinkle pepper and parsley over potatoes; stir carefully to coat potatoes evenly. Cover and refrigerate overnight. Before serving, drain off marinade.

Makes 6 servings.

Ham & Cheese Slaw

1 small head green cabbage, chopped
1 small red onion, diced
1 medium-size carrot, shredded
8 ounces Cheddar cheese, cut into
   1/2-inch cubes
8 ounces turkey ham, cut into 1/2-inch cubes
1 green bell pepper, cut into 1/2-inch pieces
1 tablespoon chopped fresh parsley
1/3 cup roasted sunflower seeds

Creamy Dressing:
1 cup plain yogurt
1/2 cup light sour cream
1/2 cup mayonnaise
2 teaspoons Dijon-style mustard
2 tablespoons fresh lemon juice
1/8 teaspoon ground allspice

Combine cabbage, onion, carrot, cheese, turkey ham, bell pepper and parsley in a large bowl.

Prepare dressing: Combine all ingredients in a small bowl. Fold into the cabbage mixture. Cover and refrigerate at least 1 hour to blend flavors. Sprinkle with sunflower kernels before serving.

Makes 8 to 10 servings.

—— Layered Cabbage Slaw ——

1 small head cabbage, shredded
4 green onions, sliced
1 green bell pepper, sliced
1 red bell pepper, sliced
1 cup shredded carrots
1/2 cup sliced ripe olives
1/2 cup chopped parsley leaves

Celery Seed Dressing:
3/4 cup cider vinegar
3/4 cup sugar
1/2 cup corn oil
1 teaspoon salt
3/4 teaspoon celery seeds
3/4 teaspoon dry mustard
1/2 teaspoon garlic powder

Layer half the cabbage, half the onions, the bell peppers, carrots, olives and parsley in a large bowl. Top with remaining cabbage and onions.

Prepare dressing: Combine all ingredients in a small saucepan and bring to a boil. Stir until sugar is dissolved. Pour hot dressing evenly over the salad. Do not toss. Cover and refrigerate at least 4 hours before serving.

Makes 8 servings.

— Smoked Lake Trout Salad —

1 (1-lb.) smoked lake trout or salmon
2 quarts bite-size mixed salad greens
4 small tomatoes, cut into wedges
4 hard-cooked eggs, shelled and quartered

Creamy Dressing:
1/2 cup light mayonnaise
1/2 cup light sour cream
1/4 cup plain yogurt
1/4 cup chili sauce
1/4 cup chopped green bell pepper
1/4 cup chopped green onion
Salt and pepper to taste

Remove skin and bones from smoked fish and break into large pieces.

Arrange salad greens on 4 plates; top each with an equal portion of the fish, tomato wedges and hard-cooked eggs. Prepare dressing: Combine all ingredients together in a small bowl. Spoon over the salad.

Makes 4 main-dish servings.

SMOKED TURKEY SALAD

1 pound smoked turkey breast, cut into strips
8 ounces Jarlsberg cheese, cut into strips
1/4 pound whole red seedless grapes
1/4 pound whole green seedless grapes
1 celery stalk, thinly sliced
1/2 cup light mayonnaise
1/2 cup light sour cream
2 to 3 tablespoons raspberry vinegar
2 teaspoons crushed green peppercorns

Combine turkey and cheese in a large bowl. Top with grapes and celery.

Combine mayonnaise, sour cream, vinegar and peppercorns in a small bowl. Spoon dressing over each serving.

Makes 4 to 6 servings.

— FETA & NAVY BEAN SALAD —

3 (1-lb.) cans navy beans, drained
1 cup (4 oz.) crumbled Wisconsin feta cheese
3/4 cup thinly sliced green onions
2 large tomatoes, diced
1/4 cup chopped fresh parsley
2 tablespoons chopped fresh dill or
    2 teaspoons dill weed
1/4 cup fresh lemon juice
1/4 cup olive oil
2 garlic cloves, minced
1/4 teaspoon freshly ground pepper
Lettuce leaves
Lemon slices and fresh dill for garnish

Combine beans, cheese, onions, tomatoes, parsley and dill in a large bowl.

Whisk lemon juice, oil, garlic and pepper in a small bowl until slightly thickened. Fold dressing into the bean mixture. Cover and refrigerate several hours to develop flavors. Serve at cool room temperature. Place a lettuce leaf on each plate. Arrange beans over lettuce. Garnish with lemon slices and dill.

Makes 8 servings.

— BUTTER-CRUMBED BROCCOLI —

3 tablespoons butter or margarine
1/2 cup finely diced red bell pepper
1 cup fresh bread crumbs
2 tablespoons chopped fresh parsley
2 tablespoons chopped fresh chives
1 teaspoon rosemary leaves
2 pounds fresh broccoli
2 or 3 tablespoons melted butter (optional)
Salt and pepper

Melt the 3 tablespoons butter in a large skillet. Add bell pepper and cook, stirring, 1 minute. Add crumbs and cook over low heat, stirring, until crumbs are toasted and browned. Remove from heat and add herbs.

Bring about 1 quart of water to a boil in a large saucepan. Cut broccoli into flowerets. Trim off woody ends of stems. Peel remaining stems and cut into 1/2-inch slices. Add broccoli to boiling water and boil, uncovered, until broccoli is crisp-tender, 4 to 5 minutes.

Drain, place into a serving dish and drizzle with melted butter, if using. Sprinkle with salt and pepper. Sprinkle with the bread crumb mixture. Serve immediately.

Makes 6 servings.

— HARVEST VEGETABLE STEW —

1 small head cauliflower, about 3/4 pound
2 medium-size potatoes, peeled and diced
2 medium-size carrots, thinly sliced
1/2 medium-size eggplant, cut into
    1/2-inch cubes
1 (1-lb.) can diced tomatoes in tomato sauce
2 medium-size onions, thinly sliced
2 medium-size zucchini, thinly sliced
2 medium-size yellow squash, thinly sliced
1/2 cup each green peas and cut green beans
1 green bell pepper, chopped
2 celery stalks, chopped
1 cup chopped fresh herbs: combination of
    dill, basil and parsley
1-1/2 cups beef broth
1/4 cup olive oil
Salt and pepper

Preheat oven to 350F (175C). Layer all of the vegetables in a 4-quart casserole dish, 1/3 at a time. Sprinkle each layer with fresh herbs.

Bring beef broth and olive oil to a boil in a medium-size saucepan and pour over the vegetables. Season with salt and pepper. Cover and bake about 1-1/2 hours or until vegetables are tender. Serve warm or at room temperature with fresh baked bread.

Makes 6 to 8 servings.

RUTABAGA CASSEROLE

2 pounds rutabagas
Salt
2 eggs, beaten
2 tablespoons all-purpose flour
2 tablespoons brown sugar
1 teaspoon salt
1/2 teaspoon grated nutmeg
3 tablespoons butter
1 cup soft bread crumbs

Peel rutabagas, cut into 1-inch pieces and cook in boiling salted water 30 minutes or until tender. Drain; place in a large bowl.

Preheat oven to 350F (175C). Butter a 2-quart casserole dish. Mash rutabagas until smooth using an electric mixer. Add eggs, flour, brown sugar, salt and nutmeg. Turn mixture into buttered casserole dish.

With tip of a wooden spoon, make 3 rows of indentations over the top of the rutabagas, about 1/2 inch apart. Dot top with butter. Sprinkle with bread crumbs. Bake 1 hour or until lightly browned.

Makes 6 to 8 servings.

TWICE-BAKED POTATOES

4 medium-size russet potatoes
1 teaspoon vegetable oil
Seasoned salt
1/2 cup dairy sour cream
1 (3-oz.) package cream cheese, softened
2 tablespoons butter or margarine
1 teaspoon garlic salt
1/2 teaspoon rosemary leaves
1/8 teaspoon freshly ground pepper
Chopped fresh parsley

Preheat oven to 400F (205C), if using. Scrub potatoes and pierce with a fork.

Rub potatoes with oil and sprinkle with seasoned salt. Arrange on a baking sheet and bake 1 hour or until soft. Or arrange in a circle in a microwave oven and cook on HIGH power 15 to 18 minutes. Cut a slice from the top of each potato. Scoop out potato pulp, leaving about a 1/4-inch shell, into a bowl. Add sour cream, cream cheese, butter, salt, rosemary and pepper to potato pulp and beat until smooth.

Spoon mixture into the potato shells. Stand the potato "lid" on top. Before serving, reheat in microwave oven on HIGH power 3 minutes, or in regular oven 10 minutes or until heated through. Sprinkle with chopped fresh parsley and serve.

Makes 4 servings.

— CRANBERRY-BANANA BREAD —

2/3 cup sugar
1/2 cup butter or margarine, softened
2 eggs
1 cup mashed ripe bananas
1 tablespoon lemon juice
2 cups all-purpose flour
1 teaspoon baking powder
1/2 teaspoon baking soda
1/2 teaspoon salt
1/2 cup dried cranberries or raisins
1 cup coarsely chopped pecans or walnuts

Preheat oven to 350F (175C). Grease a
9" × 5" loaf pan. Beat sugar, butter and
eggs in a large bowl until smooth and
light. Stir in bananas and lemon juice.

Mix flour, baking powder, soda and salt
in a small bowl. Stir dry ingredients
into creamed mixture just until blended; do not overmix. Fold in cranberries
and nuts.

Pour into greased pan and bake 50 to 60
minutes or until a wooden skewer
inserted in the center comes out clean.
Remove from pan; cool on a wire rack.

Makes 1 loaf.

SPICY ZUCCHINI BREAD

2 cups all-purpose flour
1 teaspoon each salt, baking powder, baking
   soda, cinnamon and nutmeg
3 eggs
2 cups sugar
3/4 cup vegetable oil
2 cups shredded zucchini, well drained
1-1/2 cups chopped walnuts
1/2 cup raisins
2 teaspoons vanilla extract

Preheat oven to 350F (175C). Grease and flour 2 (8" × 4") loaf pans. Sift together flour, salt, baking powder, soda, cinnamon and nutmeg in a medium-size bowl. Beat eggs in a large bowl until light; gradually beat in sugar until thick and lemon-colored. Add oil and beat well.

Stir in zucchini, nuts, raisins and vanilla. Stir in dry ingredients until moistened. Turn into greased pans. Bake 50 minutes or until a wooden skewer inserted in the centers of the loaves comes out clean. Cool 5 minutes before turning out onto a wire rack. Cool completely before slicing.

Makes 2 loaves.

— STRAWBERRY MUFFINS —

1 egg
1 cup milk
1/2 cup vegetable oil
2 cups all-purpose flour
1/3 cup sugar
1 tablespoon baking powder
1 teaspoon salt
1/4 cup strawberry jam
1/2 cup all-purpose flour
1/4 cup packed brown sugar
1/4 cup butter or margarine

Preheat oven to 400F (205C). Grease bottoms of about 12 muffin cups or line with paper baking cups. Beat egg until light and stir in milk and oil. Combine the 2 cups flour, sugar, baking powder and salt in a small bowl. Add all at once to egg mixture and stir just until flour is moistened.

Fill muffin cups about 1/3 full. Spoon 1 teaspoon strawberry jam onto batter in each cup; top with remaining batter.

Combine the 1/2 cup flour, the brown sugar and butter in a small bowl to make coarse crumbs. Sprinkle over batter in cups. Bake until golden, about 20 minutes.

Makes 12 muffins.

DRIED CHERRY SCONES

2 cups all-purpose flour
1/4 cup sugar, plus extra for sprinkling
4 teaspoons baking powder
1/8 teaspoon salt
6 tablespoons butter or margarine
1/2 cup dried cherries or dried cranberries
1/2 to 3/4 cup milk
1 egg white

Preheat oven to 450F (230C). Combine flour, sugar, baking powder and salt in a large bowl. Cut in butter until mixture resembles coarse crumbs. Add cherries.

Mix in enough milk to make a soft, but not wet, dough. Divide dough into 2 parts. On floured surface, pat out each part to a 6-inch round. Place rounds on an ungreased cookie sheet.

Brush tops of rounds with egg white and sprinkle evenly with sugar. With a straight knife, cut each round through to the bottom into 6 wedges; leave wedges in place. Bake 12 to 15 minutes or until golden-brown.

Makes 12 scones.

WILD RICE PANCAKES

1 cup cooked wild rice
2 tablespoons corn oil or melted butter
3 eggs
1-1/2 cups nonfat plain yogurt
1-1/4 cups all-purpose flour
1 teaspoon baking powder
1 tablespoon sugar
1/2 teaspoon baking soda
1/2 teaspoon salt
Butter for serving
Warm fruit or maple syrup for serving

Whisk wild rice, oil, eggs and yogurt together in a large bowl.

Combine flour, sugar, baking powder, soda and salt in a small bowl and add to the wild rice mixture.

Heat pancake griddle and grease lightly. Cook pancakes on hot griddle until bubbles form on surface. Turn and cook until golden. Serve with butter and warm fruit or maple syrup.

Makes 16 pancakes.

SAUSAGE WAFFLES

2 cups baking mix
2 eggs
1 cup milk
1 pound bulk-style breakfast sausage
3 cups peeled chopped apples
2 tablespoons butter or margarine
1 teaspoon ground cinnamon
Warm maple syrup for serving

Preheat waffle iron. With an electric mixer, beat together baking mix, eggs, milk and uncooked sausage until well blended.

Spray waffle grids with nonstick cooking spray. Spoon batter into heated waffle iron and cook 3 to 5 minutes or until golden-brown.

Meanwhile, sauté chopped apples in butter in a medium-size skillet until tender, 5 to 8 minutes. Add cinnamon. Serve waffles hot with sautéed apples and maple syrup.

Makes 6 servings.

SWEDISH POTATO LIMPA

2 medium-size potatoes, cut into pieces
2 (1/4-oz.) pkgs. active dry yeast
1/2 cup light molasses
1/4 cup butter or margarine, melted
1-1/2 teaspoons salt
2 tablespoons grated orange peel
1 tablespoon caraway seeds
1 teaspoon each anise and fennel seeds
2 cups light or medium rye flour
4 to 5 cups bread flour
Additional molasses for brushing hot loaves

Cook potatoes in 2 cups boiling water 10 to 15 minutes or until tender. Drain potatoes, reserving cooking water. Cool and mash potatoes.

Add enough water to cooking water to make 2 cups. Heat to 105 to 115F (40 to 45C). Pour into a medium-size bowl. Sprinkle yeast over water. Let stand 5 minutes or until foamy. Stir in molasses, butter, salt, orange peel, seeds and rye flour. Beat well. Beat in 2 cups bread flour until mixture is smooth. Cover and let dough rest 15 minutes. Beat in enough additional flour to make a moderately stiff dough.

Knead on a floured surface 5 to 10 minutes. Grease a bowl and add dough to the bowl. Turn dough over. Cover and let rise in a warm place until doubled. Punch down and divide into 2 parts. Shape into loaves. Place into greased 9" × 5" loaf pans. Cover and let rise until almost doubled, 45 minutes to 1 hour. Preheat oven to 350F (175C). Bake about 45 minutes. Brush with molasses and cool completely.

Makes 2 loaves.

—— ICELANDIC COFFEE BREAD ——

2 (1/4-oz.) pkgs. active dry yeast
1/2 cup warm water (105 to 115F, 40 to 45C)
1 (12-oz.) can undiluted evaporated milk
1/2 cup butter or margarine, melted
1-1/2 cups sugar
1 teaspoon salt
1-1/2 teaspoons freshly ground cardamom
2 eggs, beaten
1-1/2 cups mixed candied fruit
5 to 6 cups unbleached all-purpose flour
1/2 cup butter or margarine
1 teaspoon ground cinnamon

Dissolve yeast in water. Let stand 5 minutes or until foamy. Add milk, melted butter, 1 cup of the sugar, salt and cardamom; stir until sugar is dissolved. Add eggs, fruit and 4 cups of the flour. Beat with an electric mixer until smooth. Let stand 10 minutes.

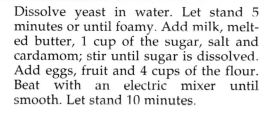

Mix in 1-1/2 cups more flour, and stir to make a stiff dough. Cover and let stand 15 minutes. Knead dough on a floured surface until smooth and elastic. Cover and let rise in a warm place until double in size, about 1 hour.

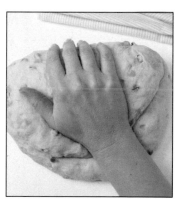

Punch dough down. Divide in half. Cut each half into 3 parts. Shape each part into a rope. Braid 3 ropes together to make a loaf. Place on lightly greased baking sheet. Cover and let rise until almost double, 45 minutes. Preheat oven to 350F (175C). Brush with melted butter. Combine remaining sugar and cinnamon; sprinkle on braids. Bake 35 to 40 minutes, or until loaves test done.

Makes 2 large braids.

GLAZED ORANGE BREAD

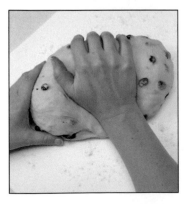

2 (1/4-oz.) pkgs. active dry yeast
About 5 cups bread flour
1 cup milk
1/2 cup sugar
1/2 cup butter or margarine
1/4 cup water
2 tablespoons grated orange peel
1 teaspoon salt
2 eggs, beaten
1 teaspoon vanilla extract
1-1/2 cups raisins

Walnut-Orange Glaze:
1 cup powdered sugar
2 teaspoons butter, softened
About 3 tablespoons orange juice
1/2 cup chopped walnuts

Combine yeast with 2 cups flour in a large mixer bowl.

Heat milk, sugar, butter, water, orange peel and salt until very warm (120F, 50C) in a small saucepan, stirring. Add to flour mixture; add eggs and vanilla. Beat on low speed 30 seconds, scraping bowl. Beat on high speed 3 minutes. Add raisins. Using a wooden spoon, stir in as much of the remaining flour as you can to make a moderately stiff dough. Cover dough and let rest 15 minutes.

Turn dough out onto a floured surface and knead 5 minutes or until smooth and elastic. Shape into a ball and place in a greased bowl; turn once. Cover dough. Let rise in a warm place until doubled, about 1-1/4 hours.

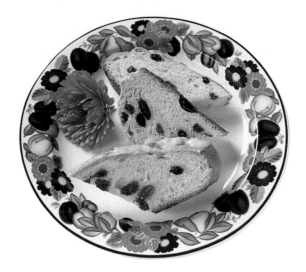

Punch down. Turn out onto a lightly greased surface. Knead 1 minute. Divide into 2 parts. Shape into round loaves. Place into 2 greased 9-inch cake pans. Cover and let rise in a warm place until doubled.

Preheat oven to 375F (190C). Make 3 diagonal slashes across the top of each loaf. Bake 40 minutes or until loaves sound hollow when tapped on bottoms. Remove from pans; cool on wire racks.

Prepare Walnut-Orange Glaze: Mix sugar, butter and orange juice until smooth; add walnuts. Spread glaze over cooled loaves.

Makes 2 loaves.

– CINNAMON-PECAN STICKY RING –

1 (1/4-oz.) pkg. active dry yeast
1/4 cup warm water (105 to 115F, 40 to 45C)
1 cup milk, scalded and cooled
1/4 cup corn oil
1/2 cup sugar
1 teaspoon salt
1 egg
3-1/2 cups all-purpose flour
1 cup chopped pecans
1/2 cup butter or margarine, melted
1/2 cup packed brown sugar

Dissolve yeast in the warm water in a large bowl. Let stand 5 minutes or until foamy. Mix in milk, oil, sugar, salt and egg. Beat in flour to make a soft, smooth dough.

Cover. Refrigerate dough 2 hours or overnight. Grease a 10-inch tube pan. Sprinkle 1/2 cup pecans over the bottom of the pan.

Pinch off walnut-size pieces of dough. Dip into melted butter, then into the brown sugar, then into butter, then into pecans and place balls of dough in bottom of tube pan arranging evenly. Cover and let rise in a warm place until almost doubled in size, about 1 hour. Preheat oven to 350F (175C). Bake 55 to 60 minutes, until golden-brown. Cool 5 minutes in pan. Invert onto a plate.

Makes 1 large ring.

POTATO ROLLS

2 (1/4-oz.) pkgs. active dry yeast
2 cups warm water (105 to 115F, 40 to 45C)
1 cup instant mashed potatoes
2/3 cup sugar
1 teaspoon salt
2 eggs, beaten
2/3 cup melted shortening or corn oil
4-1/3 cups bread flour

In a large bowl, dissolve yeast in the warm water. Stir in potatoes, sugar and salt. Let stand 5 minutes or until foamy.

Beat in eggs and shortening. Stir in flour to make a moderately stiff dough. Cover and refrigerate overnight. Punch dough down. Turn out onto a floured surface.

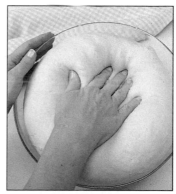

Divide into 24 balls. With floured hands, shape into rolls. Place on greased baking sheets. Cover and let rise in a warm place until nearly double in size, 30 to 45 minutes. Preheat oven to 375F (190C). Bake 15 to 20 minutes or until golden-brown.

Makes 24 rolls.

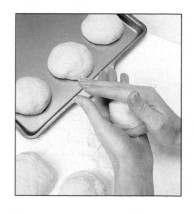

FROSTED APPLE CAKE

1 cup sugar
1/2 cup butter or margarine, softened
2 eggs, beaten
1-1/2 cups all-purpose flour
1/2 teaspoon each baking powder and
   baking soda
2 teaspoons unsweetened cocoa powder
1-1/2 teaspoons ground cinnamon
1/2 cup cold, strong coffee
3 cups chopped peeled apples
1/2 cup chopped dates
1 cup chopped walnuts or pecans

Caramel Frosting:
1/4 cup butter or margarine
1/2 cup packed brown sugar
2 tablespoons milk
3/4 to 1 cup powdered sugar, sifted

Preheat oven to 350F (175C). Butter and flour a 9- or 10-inch tube pan. Beat sugar, butter and eggs together in a large bowl until light and fluffy. Combine flour, baking powder, soda, cocoa and cinnamon in a small bowl until blended. Add to the creamed mixture with the coffee. Beat at high speed until light and fluffy. Stir in apples, dates and nuts. Spoon batter into prepared pan. Bake 45 to 50 minutes or until a wooden pick inserted in cake comes out clean. Cool in pan 10 minutes.

Prepare frosting: Combine butter, brown sugar and milk in a small saucepan. Bring to a boil, stirring. Boil 1 minute. Remove from heat and add powdered sugar; beat until smooth. Invert cake onto a plate. Drizzle frosting over cake.

Makes 12 servings.

APPLE PIE SQUARES

2 cups all-purpose flour
1/2 teaspoon salt
3/4 cup granulated sugar
1/2 cup unsalted butter or margarine
1 egg, beaten
1/2 cup dairy sour cream
1 tablespoon iced water, if necessary
1 tablespoon bread crumbs
5 large Granny Smith apples, peeled and
    sliced
Grated peel of 1 orange
1-1/2 teaspoons ground cinnamon
1/2 cup powdered sugar
1 to 2 tablespoons milk
1 teaspoon vanilla extract

Combine flour, salt and 2 tablespoons of the sugar in a food processor or large bowl. Add butter and process until mixture resembles coarse crumbs. Combine egg and sour cream in a small bowl. Add to flour mixture, mixing until dough forms; add water if necessary. Form dough into a ball.

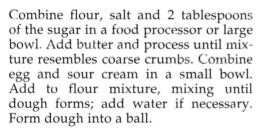

Preheat oven to 375F (190C). Grease and flour a 13" × 9" baking pan. Cut dough into 2 parts. Roll out 1 part to fit pan. Fit into the pan, patching dough if necessary. Sprinkle bottom crust with crumbs. Combine apples, orange peel, 1/2 cup of the sugar and the cinnamon in a large bowl. Fill crust with apples.

Roll out remaining dough; place over apples. Seal edges. Brush top with water and sprinkle with remaining sugar. Bake 50 minutes or until brown. Combine powdered sugar, milk and vanilla and drizzle over pastry. Cool and cut into squares.

Makes 12 squares.

—— BLUEBERRY CREAM PIE ——

1 (8-oz.) package cream cheese, softened
2 cups whipping cream
1/2 cup sugar
1 teaspoon fresh lemon juice
1 (9-inch) baked pastry shell
1 cup blueberry jam
2 tablespoons powdered sugar
2 cups fresh blueberries
Lemon peel strips for decoration

With an electric mixer, beat cream cheese, 1/2 cup of the cream, the sugar and lemon juice until light. Pour creamy mixture into the pie shell. Spread with blueberry jam.

Beat remaining cream in a medium-size bowl until soft peaks form. Beat in the powdered sugar. Reserve some berries for decoration. Fold in remaining blueberries and spread mixture over the pie. Cover and refrigerate 2 to 4 hours before serving. Cut into small slices because the pie is very rich. Garnish with reserved berries and lemon peel.

Makes 10 to 12 servings.

— Cardamom Sugar Cookies —

1/2 cup butter, softened
1/2 cup sugar
1 egg
1/2 cup corn oil
1 teaspoon freshly ground cardamom seeds
2-1/4 cups all-purpose flour
1/2 teaspoon baking soda
1/2 teaspoon cream of tartar
1/4 teaspoon salt

With an electric mixer, cream butter, sugar and egg until light and fluffy. Beat in oil.

Add remaining ingredients and mix well. Form into a ball. Cover and refrigerate until dough is chilled.

Preheat oven to 375F (190C). Cover cookie sheets with parchment paper or waxed paper. Shape dough into 1-inch balls. Place on prepared cookie sheet. Flatten with a glass dipped in sugar. Bake 10 minutes or until cookies are firm to the touch and lightly browned around the edges.

Makes 48 cookies.

FUDGE LAYER CAKE

1 cup (6 oz.) semisweet chocolate chips, melted with 1/2 cup hot water, cooled
1 teaspoon vanilla extract
2 cups all-purpose flour
1 teaspoon each baking soda and salt
1/2 cup butter or margarine, softened
1-1/4 cups sugar
3 eggs
3/4 cup milk

Fudge Frosting:
1/2 cup whipping cream
1 cup semisweet chocolate chips
1 cup granulated sugar
1 cup powdered sugar, sifted
1 teaspoon vanilla extract

Preheat oven to 350F (175C). Grease and flour 2 (9-inch) cake pans. Combine chocolate and vanilla.

Stir flour, soda and salt together in a small bowl. With an electric mixer, cream butter and sugar; beat in eggs until light and fluffy. Add flour mixture and milk; beat until batter is smooth. Blend in chocolate mixture. Pour into prepared pans. Bake 30 to 35 minutes or until cake springs back when pressed in center. Cool 10 minutes. Remove from pans and cool on a wire rack.

Prepare frosting: Bring cream to a boil. Remove from heat; stir in chocolate until melted. Add granulated sugar, return to heat. Bring to a boil; boil 2 minutes, stirring. Remove from heat. Beat in powdered sugar and vanilla until frosting is smooth. Fill and frost the cake layers with the frosting.

Makes about 12 servings.

—— LAYERED FILBERT BARS ——

1 cup filberts (hazelnuts)
2 cups all-purpose flour
1-1/2 cups packed brown sugar
1 cup butter or margarine, softened
2 eggs
1 teaspoon vanilla extract
1 tablespoon all-purpose flour
1/2 teaspoon baking powder
1/4 teaspoon salt
1 cup flaked coconut
1/2 cup chopped dates

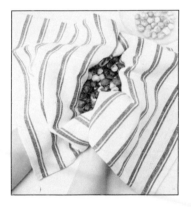

Preheat oven to 350F (175F). Spread filberts in a shallow pan and toast in oven 4 to 5 minutes. Cool. Rub off skins using a towel. Chop nuts and set aside.

Grease a 13" × 9" baking pan. With 2 knives or a pastry blender, combine flour, 1 cup of the brown sugar and the butter in a medium-size bowl until mixture makes soft crumbs. Press half the crumb mixture into the bottom of prepared pan. Bake 10 to 15 minutes or until lightly browned.

Beat eggs, vanilla, remaining 1/2 cup brown sugar, flour, baking powder and salt in a medium-size bowl until light and fluffy. Stir in coconut, dates and half the chopped nuts. Spread mixture over baked crust. Mix remaining nuts with remaining crumb mixture. Sprinkle over the filling. Bake 25 to 30 minutes until golden. Cool in pan. Cut into bars.

Makes 36 bars.

— EASY CHOCOLATE TRUFFLES —

1 cup unsalted butter
2 (7-oz.) milk chocolate bars with
    almonds, chopped
2-1/2 cups quick-cooking rolled oats
About 1 cup powdered sugar, sifted

Melt butter in a glass bowl in a microwave oven on HIGH power 1 to 2 minutes; add chocolate bars. Stir until chocolate is melted.

Blend oats into chocolate. Refrigerate until mixture can be shaped into balls. Line a baking sheet or tray with waxed paper. With a small ice cream scoop or a tablespoon, form mixture into round balls. Mixture will be crumbly, but it will hold together in balls. Place on lined pan and refrigerate to firm.

Roll in powdered sugar. Store in refrigerator, but bring to room temperature 30 minutes before serving.

Makes about 50.

RHUBARB CUSTARD PIE

4 cups chopped fresh rhubarb
   (1/2-inch pieces)
3/4 cup sugar
2 tablespoons all-purpose flour
1 tablespoon fresh lemon juice
1/8 teaspoon salt
1 unbaked 9-inch pie shell
3 eggs
1 cup half and half or undiluted
   evaporated milk
1 teaspoon freshly grated nutmeg
2 tablespoons sugar
Mint sprigs for decoration

Preheat oven to 400F (205C). Mix rhubarb, sugar, flour, lemon juice and salt in a large bowl. Turn into pie shell. Bake 20 minutes. Beat eggs, half and half, nutmeg and sugar in a medium-size bowl until well mixed. Pour over the hot rhubarb in the pie shell.

Bake 10 minutes. Sprinkle with sugar and bake 10 minutes longer until top of pie is browned. Cool completely before cutting. Decorate with mint sprigs.

Makes 6 to 8 servings.

— RHUBARB-STRAWBERRY CRISP —

4 cups chopped fresh rhubarb
1 pint (2 cups) fresh whole
   strawberries, sliced
1-1/2 cups sugar
1 cup all-purpose flour
1 teaspoon baking powder
1/4 teaspoon salt
1 egg, beaten
1/2 cup butter or margarine, melted

Preheat oven to 350F (175C). Butter a 9-inch-square baking pan. Mix rhubarb, strawberries and 1/2 cup sugar in a large bowl.

Turn mixture into prepared pan. Combine flour, remaining sugar, the baking powder, salt and egg in a medium-size bowl. Mix until crumbly.

Sprinkle crumbly mixture over fruit. Drizzle with melted butter. Bake 45 to 55 minutes or until browned. Serve with whipped cream or ice cream.

Makes 8 to 10 servings.

RICE PUDDING

1/2 cup short-grain rice
1 cup water
4 cups milk
3 eggs, beaten
2/3 cup sugar
2 teaspoons vanilla extract
2 tablespoons butter or margarine, melted
1/4 teaspoon salt
About 1 teaspoon ground cinnamon

Raspberry Sauce:
1 quart fresh or frozen raspberries
1-3/4 cups water
1 cup sugar
2-1/2 tablespoons cornstarch

Combine rice and water in a small saucepan. Bring to a boil. Reduce heat to low and simmer until water is absorbed. Add milk and cook until rice is tender, about 30 minutes.

Preheat oven to 350F (175C). Butter a 2-1/2-quart baking dish. Combine eggs, sugar, vanilla, butter and salt in a small bowl. Add rice to buttered dish and stir in egg mixture. Sprinkle liberally with cinnamon. Place dish into a large pan of hot water. Bake 50 to 60 minutes or until pudding is set. Remove from the hot water and cool on a rack.

Prepare sauce: Bring berries and water to a boil. Combine sugar and cornstarch in a small bowl. Stir sugar mixture into boiling berry mixture and cook until thickened, stirring. Refrigerate leftovers.

Makes 8 to 10 servings.

— TOASTED OATMEAL COOKIES —

1/2 cup butter, margarine or shortening
1/2 cup packed brown sugar
1/2 cup granulated sugar
1 teaspoon vanilla extract
1 egg
3/4 cup all-purpose flour
1 teaspoon ground cinnamon
1/2 teaspoon each baking powder and
   baking soda
1/4 teaspoon salt
1-1/2 cups rolled oats, toasted
1/2 cup chopped walnuts

Preheat oven to 350F (175C). In a large bowl, beat butter, brown sugar, granulated sugar, vanilla and egg until light and fluffy. Add flour, cinnamon, baking powder, soda and salt. Blend well. Stir in toasted oats and walnuts.

Drop by rounded teaspoonfuls 2 inches apart onto greased baking sheets. Bake 10 to 12 minutes or until golden-brown. Remove from baking sheets and cool on a wire rack.

Makes about 40 cookies.

TOSCA CAKE

1 cup whipping cream
2 eggs
1 teaspoon vanilla extract
1-1/2 cups all-purpose flour
1 cup sugar
2 teaspoons baking powder
1/4 teaspoon salt
1/3 cup butter or margarine
1/3 cup sugar
3/4 cup sliced almonds
1 tablespoon all-purpose flour
1 tablespoon milk

Preheat oven to 350F (175C). Butter a 10-inch springform pan.

In large bowl, beat cream until stiff; beat in eggs and vanilla. Combine flour, sugar, baking powder and salt in a small bowl. Add to cream mixture and beat until smooth. Pour into prepared pan. Bake 40 minutes or until cake pulls away from side of pan.

While cake bakes, prepare topping: Melt butter in a small saucepan. Add remaining topping ingredients, and bring to a boil, stirring constantly. Continue stirring until thickened, 4 to 5 minutes. Pour over hot cake, completely covering top. Bake 15 to 20 minutes longer or until golden-brown. Serve warm or cold.

Makes 8 to 10 servings.

Metric Chart

Comparison to Metric Measure					Fahrenheit to Celsius	
When You Know	Symbol	Multiply By	To Find	Symbol	F	C
teaspoons	tsp	5.0	milliliters	ml	200—205	95
tablespoons	tbsp	15.0	milliliters	ml	220—225	105
fluid ounces	fl. oz.	30.0	milliliters	ml	245—250	120
cups	c	0.24	liters	l	275	135
pints	pt.	0.47	liters	l	300—305	150
quarts	qt.	0.95	liters	l	325—330	165
ounces	oz.	28.0	grams	g	345—350	175
pounds	lb.	0.45	kilograms	kg	370—375	190
Fahrenheit	F	5/9 (after subtracting 32)	Celsius	C	400—405	205
					425—430	220
					445—450	230
					470—475	245
					500	260

Liquid Measure to Milliliters

1/4 teaspoon	=	1.25 milliliters
1/2 teaspoon	=	2.5 milliliters
3/4 teaspoon	=	3.75 milliliters
1 teaspoon	=	5.0 milliliters
1-1/4 teaspoons	=	6.25 milliliters
1-1/2 teaspoons	=	7.5 milliliters
1-3/4 teaspoons	=	8.75 milliliters
2 teaspoons	=	10.0 milliliters
1 tablespoon	=	15.0 milliliters
2 tablespoons	=	30.0 milliliters

Liquid Measure to Liters

1/4 cup	=	0.06 liters
1/2 cup	=	0.12 liters
3/4 cup	=	0.18 liters
1 cup	=	0.24 liters
1-1/4 cups	=	0.3 liters
1-1/2 cups	=	0.36 liters
2 cups	=	0.48 liters
2-1/2 cups	=	0.6 liters
3 cups	=	0.72 liters
3-1/2 cups	=	0.84 liters
4 cups	=	0.96 liters
4-1/2 cups	=	1.08 liters
5 cups	=	1.2 liters
5-1/2 cups	=	1.32 liters

INDEX